Powerful. Beautiful. Compelling! I'm so thankful that Kevin wrote this book. Read it too. It will help you to choose and to offer the love of God.

STASI ELDREDGE
Author of *Captivating* and *Becoming Myself*

In *Choose and Choose Again*, Kevin Butcher paints moving portraits of brokenness and healing. Kevin draws upon his own journey from despair to hope and faithfully recounts how the love of God has resurrected others. *Choose and Choose Again* is about life-and-death struggle to truly know that we are loved. Savor these stories, and taste of the deep love the Father has for you.

JEFF MANION
Senior pastor at Ada Bible Church in Grand Rapids, Michigan, and author of *The Land Between* and *Satisfied*

This book is beautiful. A truly authentic and powerful revelation of the deepest hunger of our heart met by the strongest force in the universe—love. May you read it and weep, and then have the courage to choose it for yourself.

DANIELLE STRICKLAND
Speaker, advocate, and author

The book you hold in your hands is dangerous. It is dangerous because it passionately and convincingly speaks to God's love for his children—for you! First it strips you down to your own emptiness, desire for love, and the false beliefs that you are not worthy. Then it slowly builds you back up with the deep, abiding sense of the relentless and gracious love of God. *Choose and Choose Again* is a rare book that perfectly captures the character and voice of its author and forces you to grapple with stories—Kevin's, those he writes about, and your own. This is one of the best and most transformative books on the love of God I know about.

KEN WYTSMA
Lead pastor at Antioch in Bend, Oregon, and author of *The Grand Paradox: The Messiness of Life, the Mystery of God and the Necessity of Faith*

One of the best life-changing books I've read in a while. In *Choose and Choose Again*, J. Kevin Butcher writes with vulnerability and the raw emotion of one on the brink of suicide until he finds healing in the power of God's love. His story, along with others, resonates with our greatest hurt and deepest need—to know we matter. I wept over my own wounds and rejoiced in the restorative power of God's sincere love for me. I'm convinced you will experience the same.

MICCA CAMPBELL
Speaker and author of *An Untroubled Heart: Finding a Faith That Is Stronger Than All My Fears*

Kevin Butcher has pulled together a collection of beautiful stories—including his own—that powerfully reminds us of the Father's passionate, persistent love for us. It's clear that

Kevin, as a faithful pastor, has a unique capacity to serve as a conduit for that love in a way that transforms the most unexpected lives. Be blessed and encouraged by God's work in and through him!

DR. JOSEPH M. STOWELL
President of Cornerstone University in Grand Rapids, Michigan

Wow! I felt enlightened, heartbroken, empowered, and overjoyed as I read chapter after chapter about the love of the Father meeting broken and wounded people. Real talk for real people seeking real help for real problems from a real Father! Our choice to choose the Father's unconditional, radical love and live it out in the community of faith takes courage, but it will help us live the life he has designed for us. Read and see what a difference his love makes in the lives of everyday, ordinary, struggling, and hurting people who choose to accept his love.

REV. LAWRENCE C. GLASS, JR.
President of the Council of Baptist Pastors of Detroit, Michigan

Millions all over the world long to experience the authentic love described in *Choose and Choose Again*. Let these remarkable stories convince you that God has also made it possible for you to choose this incredible life.

DR. BRUCE McNICOL
President of Trueface and bestselling coauthor of *The Cure* and *The Cure & Parents*

Not since Manning's *The Ragamuffin Gospel* have I read paragraphs that so connect me to the Father's love and grace. Don't think of *Choose and Choose Again* as a book. Think of it as God whispering comfort and love into your heart when what you have done or what has been done against you wakes you up in the middle of the night in a cold sweat of fear and doubt.

ED UNDERWOOD, THM, DD
Pastor at Church of the Open Door and author of *When God Breaks Your Heart, Reborn to Be Wild,* and *The Trail*

I could not put down this book! Why? It is biblical, honest, riveting, heart-rending, and hopeful. As I read the stories in *Choose and Choose Again*, I cried, I laughed, I prayed, and I healed. Kevin has been my close friend for decades, and I know firsthand that he has tasted the love of the Father deeply and very personally, and it has healed him . . . and it will heal you! I'll be recommending this book to my church family because I love them.

THE REVEREND CARLTON P. HARRIS, TH.M.

CHOOSE + CHOOSE AGAIN

CHOOSE

+

CHOOSE AGAIN

THE BRAVE ACT OF RETURNING TO GOD'S LOVE
J. KEVIN BUTCHER

A NavPress resource published in alliance
with Tyndale House Publishers, Inc.

NavPress is the publishing ministry of The Navigators, an international Christian organization and leader in personal spiritual development. NavPress is committed to helping people grow spiritually and enjoy lives of meaning and hope through personal and group resources that are biblically rooted, culturally relevant, and highly practical.

For more information, visit www.NavPress.com.

Choose and Choose Again: The Brave Act of Returning to God's Love

Copyright © 2016 by J. Kevin Butcher. All rights reserved.

A NavPress resource published in alliance with Tyndale House Publishers, Inc.

NAVPRESS and the NAVPRESS logo are registered trademarks of NavPress, The Navigators, Colorado Springs, CO. *TYNDALE* is a registered trademark of Tyndale House Publishers, Inc. Absence of ® in connection with marks of NavPress or other parties does not indicate an absence of registration of those marks.

The Team:
Don Pape, Publisher
Caitlyn Carlson, Acquisitions Editor, Development Editor
Alyssa Force, Designer

Cover photograph copyright © Paul McGee/Getty Images. All rights reserved.

Library of Congress Cataloging-in-Publication Data

Names: Butcher, J. Kevin, author.
Title: Choose and choose again : the brave act of returning to God's love /
  J. Kevin Butcher.
Description: Colorado Springs : NavPress, 2016.
Identifiers: LCCN 2016015615 (print) | LCCN 2016030733 (ebook) | ISBN
  9781631465246 | ISBN 9781631465277 (Apple) | ISBN 9781631465253
  (E-Pub) |
  ISBN 9781631465260 (Kindle)
Subjects: LCSH: God (Christianity—Love.
Classification: LCC BT140 .B88 2016 (print) | LCC BT140 (ebook) | DDC
  248.4—dc23
LC record available at https://lccn.loc.gov/2016015615

ISBN 978-1-63146-524-6

Printed in the United States of America

22	21	20	19	18	17	16
7	6	5	4	3	2	1

To Carla—the love of my life.

CONTENTS

ACKNOWLEDGMENTS

FOUR YEARS AGO, my wife, Carla, and I sat on the Jacobsons' back porch in Bend, Oregon, and Don Jacobson asked me what I would write about if I were given the opportunity. I told him that without question I would write about the healing power of the love of God—because his love not only had saved my life but was powerfully healing many broken human beings in our faith community in Detroit.

Thanks, Don, for encouraging me to turn those healing stories into a book of hope for those who are dying on the inside because they haven't yet experienced that same love. And thanks to the team at D. C. Jacobson and Associates for their early professional nurture as this healing project began to take shape.

The intimate and relational ethos of NavPress is a perfect fit for these stories about the love of God. Thank you, NavPress team, for your tireless work on our behalf. And Don Pape, you are a man I have learned to call my brother. Thank you for believing in the love and grace of God enough to take a risk on our book and for weeping with me over its healing message. You're a gifted publisher, but more than that, you're a lover of people. Please . . . never change.

After I found out the book was seriously too long, I panicked for a moment and wondered what kind of editor would be able to shave so many words without inadvertently slicing the life out of these healing stories. Caitlyn Carlson, you did it. You allowed yourself to be touched by the painful and redemptive journeys of human beings you had never met. With tireless empathy, you felt my heart at every turn, and you patiently answered every question. It was you, gifted daughter of God, more than any other, who helped make this book what it was intended to be.

From our first phone call, Robin Bermel, I sensed that you weren't just doing your job but that you connected personally with the core message of this project. Thanks to you and the entire Tyndale marketing team for doing what you do best—with intensity—to get this message into the hands of those who desperately long to know they are loved.

To my friends Ed Underwood and Bill Brewer—where would I be today if not for your constant, tangible expressions of the love of God in my life over the last thirty-five years? Your influence is felt in every breath of my healing story. And how many times would I have quit, Dave Burchett, if not for your brotherly words, spoken over and over?—"The message of God's healing love must get out."

Whether you know it or not, Sean Hogan Downey, you have been my mentor for most of the last two decades! So much of what you have taught me is in the very fiber and fabric of this book.

Carlton Harris, Carol Brewer, Nathan Mains, Judy Underwood, Larry Glass, Bob and Gretchen Worcester, Chuck McCoskey, Harvey Carey, and Prince Mntambo—you have all helped brother and sister me into maturity and prepared my heart for the humbling task of sensitively recording these hope-filled, healing stories. You are in my heart forever.

To Pastors Pam Pangborn, Joe Herd, and Rita Beale, and the staff and deacon board of Hope Community Church—my deep and passionate thanks for allowing me the time to write and for shepherding the body of Christ in my occasional absence. You are by far the most authentic and deeply Jesus-loving group of leaders I have been privileged to work alongside in thirty-three years of pastoral ministry.

Audrey Brennan and Sue Lubinski, you are not only two of my dearest friends but also my heroes. Thank you for courageously wrestling with the love of God every day—and for also finding time and energy to organize me in this process. God knows this book would have gone nowhere without you. And Sally Stump—my amazing mother-in-law—you told me for years to write a book. I finally listened.

This project was nurtured in the safe and loving relationships of Hope Community Church of Detroit. I love each of you more than words can express. To my Boyz to Men leaders and brothers at Hope—it is a privilege to fight the battle for the healing of the sons and daughters of God . . . together.

To the Evangelical Covenant Church—the most Jesus-like and radically loving denomination on the planet—thanks for taking a chance on us at Hope so many years ago and for believing in us still.

But I clearly owe a special debt to the courage and vision of Brian, Kennell, Melissa, Samson, Sophia, June, Elle, Nikola, Cindy, Audrey, Marc, Keith, and Lory. Thank you for choosing over and over again to surrender to the Father's love, and also for bravely and compassionately choosing to allow me to tell your healing story. A special thanks to my dad and mom for your gracious and unselfish permission to disclose a piece of your journey. And to the unnamed brother in chapter 3, to Eddie, and to my friend Dan—rest in peace, dear brothers, until we meet again in the loving arms of Jesus.

Finally, a word to my family: Andrea, Leigh Anne, and Caroline, you aren't just in my heart. You *are* my heart. "And if I ever lost you, how much would I cry . . ." From your childhood, I have watched you eagerly receive and lavishly give away Abba's love. I see Jesus in you. I am so proud. Dusty and John, I love you like the sons I never had. Your love for my daughters and grandchildren is one of the great gifts in my life. You are strong brothers. You are healers. I am humbled to walk by your side. And precious Ada, thank you for the gift of "good church" and, along with little Mack, for letting me be your Papa.

Carla, your love is the single most convincing proof to me that there is a personal loving God who loves me, too. You are my best friend, my partner, my soul. I will love you until the end of time.

Abba, centuries ago, your love delivered me through Jesus Christ. In 1990, on a dark freeway in Detroit, your love delivered me once again. Today, your unconditional love surrounds me, secures me, and continues to heal me. I long for the day when I will see you—and experience your love—face-to-face.

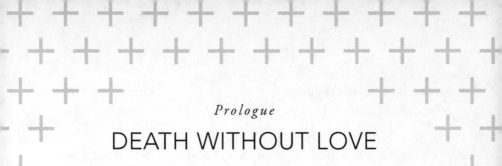

DEATH WITHOUT LOVE

Late have I loved you . . . In my unlovely state, I plunged
into those lovely created things which you made. You were
with me, and I was not with you . . . You touched me, and
I am set on fire to attain the peace which is yours.
ST. AUGUSTINE, *Confessions*

I still haven't found
What I'm looking for.
U2, *The Joshua Tree*

I WANTED TO DIE.

Driving down I-94 that night on the east side of metro Detroit, I was suddenly overwhelmed by the impulse to veer into the cement embankment of the Allard overpass to silence the screaming emptiness in my spirit. There had been an agonizingly vacant cavern in my soul for thirty-five years, but I didn't have a clue how to make the pain go away.

It sure wasn't for lack of trying. Achievement was my drug of choice for almost four decades. Athletically I was moderately gifted but worked really hard to make up in effort what I lacked in raw talent. When I finally received notice I had been named a 1975 NAIA Division III Football All-American, the emptiness in my gut was bathed in a morphine-like hit of achievement and approval. But thirty seconds later, the pain started screaming again.

It was the same story with academics. I'm certainly no genius, but I labored intensely and excelled at every level from grade school through a rigorous four-year master's degree in theology at Dallas Theological Seminary. Co-receiving the Charles A. Nash Historical Theology award in front of a gallery of my fellow fourth-year DTS students gave me a euphoric high—until it didn't.

And spiritually? Overachieving rule-keeper, that was me. Growing up, I was a Bible-reader, verse-memorizer, parent-obeyer, youth-group leader, and no-booze-sex-or-drugs, six-times-a-week church-attender. Look, I'm not saying those are bad things. But this rule-keeping was my identity—and it never, ever quieted the howling emptiness in my spirit. My Christianity was always about performance. *Hey, I'm the chaplain of my college class, I speak to church youth groups about Jesus, and do you know I've led dozens to believe in him?* And later, *I'm a pastor of a church—did you like the sermon I preached last week? I'm dying for someone to tell me that I matter, that I'm enough.* But none of the performances, sermons, articles, or counseling sessions *were* enough to fill the inner emptiness for more than a moment.

So now I found myself with what looked like the perfect life—married to the woman of my dreams, father to three beautiful daughters, pastoring a historic church that was coming back to life, watching people trust in Christ, landing speaking engagements and approval for my teaching and leadership and courage . . .

And I still just wanted to die.

I'd love to say I heard a voice, saw a vision, or had some kind of supernatural impression of God's great plans for me to be healed and save the world. But I'm still not entirely sure why I didn't jerk the wheel of my car toward the concrete barrier that promised to stop the weeping in my tortured, empty spiritual heart. All I remember is the grace of God pressing the faces of my three little girls—Andrea, Leigh Anne, and Caroline—into my suicidal consciousness. I saw them looking at me, depending on me, loving me—often despite myself. And I couldn't bear the thought of those three precious lives dealing with the legacy of a dad who wouldn't face his pain and chose to pass it on to them instead.

So, shocked and confused, I limped to the next exit and found my way home to my family. But that night, like the prodigal son in Luke 15, I hit bottom. After a long, long journey in my particular version of the "far country"—through one terrifying "I don't want to live anymore" moment of grace—I finally came to my senses. Don't get me wrong. There was no immediate epiphany of deep theological truth or insight. But that night, I came face-to-face with a reality that had taken me years to confront: my own inner emptiness and my absolute inability to fill it. I couldn't live with that emptiness any longer. If I didn't find a way to be whole, to be secure, to be at peace, I was already dead.

I first believed in Jesus when I was five years old, sitting in a small church in northern Indiana one winter evening as the pastor told us about the One who loved us enough to die in our place. While most kids my age were ripping the pages out of the hymnbook, I actually heard the guy and got it and believed. From that moment on, I had a relationship with God. I was forgiven. To use the evangelical buzzword—but also a favorite word of Paul's—I was saved. But in terms of a relationship, that was as far as it had ever gone. Before now.

After that night on the freeway, in those few days of post-trauma clarity, I asked God to show me the way, to show me what to do or what not to do to fill up the emptiness inside.

What I remember next is finding myself with a book in my hands—Brennan Manning's *The Ragamuffin Gospel*—and then reading and sobbing from a place deep within. It was suddenly so clear: The emptiness in my spirit was meant to be filled with the personal, unconditional, experiential, deep and long, wide and high love of Jesus Christ. It was this love, *his* love, that I had always known about in my head but had never, ever experienced in my life or heart or emotions or spirit. I had preached about this love to thousands of people, all the while having no idea that he really, personally loved me. I had for years and years been a travel agent "handing out brochures to places [I had] never visited."[1] The howling agony that launched me into a thirty-year addiction to achievement, approval, and applause—the pain that almost ripped my life from my wife and girls on an urban freeway—was Augustine's God-shaped vacuum. My spirit simply longed to hear my heavenly Father say, "I love you, son. I truly, freely, unconditionally, and forever just . . . love . . . you."

So I tried something novel. I asked the God who said that he loved me to show me what was going on. And then I asked him, "Please, I beg you, show me the way."

That's how my journey began—a journey to wholeness, fullness, and freedom, to knowing the love of Christ that fills us with all the fullness of God (Ephesians 3:17-19).

+ + +

Most—and I really mean most—of the believers I have met and served over the last twenty years in Africa, Europe, and South America; in the suburbs, cities, and rural areas of the United States; and in the rough urban neighborhood of Detroit where I pastor now are filled with this same kind of emptiness. It's not about color or ethnicity or money or poverty or gender or age or education or denomination. It's about the human soul. God longs to fill us with his love, but the enemy wants to convince us that we can be filled with anything and everything else.

In my experience, the biggest issue in the body of Christ today is not that believers don't love God—but that we aren't really sure he loves us. And if Jesus' words in John 13 are true, then knowing and experiencing this love in the depths of our spirit is the most important reality of all.

Do you remember some of his last words to his core group of eleven followers just before he died? "A new commandment I give you, that you love one another, *as I have loved you*. Because if you love one another, all will know that you are my followers" (John 13:34-35, author's paraphrase). This isn't plan B or a sidebar quest of the Christian experience. If we don't first take his love into our own hearts, then we have no love to give. And the world doesn't see him. Or believe in him. Or know him. If I understand Jesus correctly, knowing the love of Christ is everything. And you know what the Greek word for "everything" means? Yeah—everything.

If love is the core of God's character and the very heart of his relationship with us, we shouldn't be surprised to find his love *everywhere* in the biblical story. God didn't just talk about his love in Deuteronomy and leave it at that. He came back in Ruth with the story of his redemptive love through Boaz and once again in the Song of Solomon with epic poetry about his love. In Hosea we read the story of God's love for us even when we sleep around on him, and we see in Isaiah that God tattoos our names on the palms of his hands. Over and over in all four gospels Jesus loves us through each human encounter, and in Romans we read that "God commends his own love toward us, in that while we were yet sinners, Christ died for us" (Romans 5:8, WEB). Later in the same letter, Paul passionately reminds us to call God "Abba" (8:15), the cry of a child for their beloved Father, and says that "nothing can ever separate us from his love" (8:38, TLB). Paul's still not done—he comes back with powerful doses of God's love in Ephesians, Philippians, and Colossians. And then Peter comforts us with the bottom-line truth that "love covers a multitude of sins" (1 Peter 4:8, NLT).

Apparently God thought we couldn't read it enough, hear it enough, discuss it enough, or experience it enough. In fact, John tells us in his first letter, "God *is* love" (1 John 4:8, emphasis added). If we don't get the truth about his love for us, not just in our heads but deep down in our spirits, then nothing else really matters. With his love, we truly live. Without the experience of his love, we're empty—and have already begun to die.

Listen, my story isn't unique. It's the human story. We're all born with a deadly emptiness in our spirits that cries out to be filled with the Father's love. Perhaps you've come face-to-face with this emptiness in your own heart. Don't despair. Because I promise, God is pursuing *you* and calling out to *you* with his love. But if you're in that place where you can't quite yet hear his voice—well, this book is full of real, raw stories of other painfully empty sons and daughters who are finally experiencing a grace that is now bringing them home to his healing love. I'm praying you will let these brothers and sisters give you hope that *you* don't need to live empty anymore, that his love for *you* is very real and very near. That you will let their stories give you courage to bravely choose—and choose again—to allow his love to bring *you* home.

Chapter 1

THE POWER OF LOVE

Sometimes I am frightened
But I'm ready to learn 'bout the power of love.
JENNIFER RUSH, "THE POWER OF LOVE"

Love covers a multitude of sins.
PETER, 1 PETER 4:8, NLT

"WILL YOU GO SEE HIM?"

Christine came up to me after church, fidgeting nervously.

Him was her ex-husband, Dan Schoenfeld—#227495 in the Macomb County Jail.

"Of course," I said, not really sure what I was getting myself into. I was still a rookie when it came to experiencing the love of God in my own wounded heart. Did I have what it takes to love another profoundly broken brother—like Dan?

A few days later I sat down across from an angry, scary, tattooed, muscled, 225-pound inmate whose glare shouted, *You're wasting my time, you sissy Bible thumper. I've got no use for your religion or your god.* His hands and feet were chained, but it didn't matter. My heart was in my throat, and my gut was churning. This wasn't going to go well.

There was good reason for all the hate I was feeling in the room. As a child, Dan was consistently and brutally beaten by his alcoholic father. Dan's dad also beat his mom, and Dan constantly got in between her and his father, thinking that if he wasn't there to defend her, she was going to die. At the age of eight, Dan started shoplifting and then breaking into homes and stealing whatever he could get his hands on. He loved the thrill of getting away with petty crimes but also secretly hoped that he would get caught. Maybe then his dad would start paying attention to him in some kind of positive way.

Later Dan began partying, drinking, and drugging— and after a failed first marriage where his wife cheated on him with his best friend, he started shooting heroin to try to numb the pain. His depression, anger, and emptiness increased until one day he tried to kill himself with that same mind-numbing heroin—but he woke up eight hours after tying off his arm and injecting the poison, his body literally blue. He didn't care about anyone or anything because in his mind, no one, including God, cared about him.

At the end of his second failed marriage, this time to Christine, Dan's violence escalated. He silently broke into a neighbor's home, threatened a woman with a broken broomstick handle that he used to simulate a gun, and raped her. And then he ran. He lived a couple of more tortured years in

Florida, angry and paranoid, always looking over his shoulder, until the system finally caught up with him and brought him back to Michigan to face the rape charge.

Sitting across from him at a bolted-down prison table, I opened the Bible—to John's gospel, I think—and began to speak a little of the good news of Jesus. Dan didn't say a word. He just stared at me. He wasn't having any of it. After about ten minutes, I knew the visit was a failure.

Closing the Bible, I began to silently ask God, *What now, Father? What do you want me to do?* And then it happened. As I looked down at the prison-gray tabletop, my heart began to break for the broken human being sitting across from me. As tears came to my eyes, ran down my nose, and hit the gray surface, I began to love this brother who obviously hated me. Almost without thinking, I walked around the table, threw my arms around Dan's neck, whispered in his ear that I loved him, kissed him on the cheek, and asked him if I could come back.

"Yeah," he said. "Come back if you want." He told me later that in the moment he wasn't sure why he responded the way he did.

As I walked out of the jail, I mentally beat the heck out of myself. *Why did you kiss him? And fine, tell him that you love him in the name of God or Jesus or the church or whatever, but did you need to whisper it IN HIS EAR?* I had acted like a fool in front of a rock-hard felon who obviously needed something I didn't have to give.

Little did I know that when Dan went back to his cube that day, his knees buckled like a prize fighter who had taken one too many blows to the head. His heart and spirit were rocked by the raw power of the love of God. He said to himself, "What just happened to me? No one has ever hugged me like that. No man has ever kissed me and told me he loves me. And no one has ever cried over me. Not over someone like me. Please, God, if there is a God, I've got to have more of what just happened in that room." And so began Dan's journey to the arms of the Father.

Eight years later, at the Lakeland Correctional Facility in Coldwater, Michigan, almost a decade into a fourteen- to forty-two-year prison sentence for rape, Dan Schoenfeld—a man so wounded and broken that he hated the world and would just as soon beat you as he would speak with you—bowed his heart to the love of God and put his trust in Jesus.

What melted the steel in his soul? What began to heal the wound? What overcame the abuse and the rage-filled defense and the pain? The power of the love of a God who reveals himself in Jesus Christ. Just as one of Jesus' main followers Peter once said—this love "covers a multitude of sins" (1 Peter 4:8, NLT). Peter should know. He was the guy who denied he even knew Jesus, right when Jesus needed him most. And a few weeks later, Jesus powerfully loved Peter back to life—because that's what the love of Jesus always does.

I didn't plan to weep over Dan. The love of God compelled me to beyond reason. I was barely in the beginning stages of realizing God's love for me personally, and yet that same love was already pumping through my slowly healing heart into the heart and life of another of God's wounded sons.

That same love followed Dan through all eighteen years in the Michigan correctional system. It began to break him at Jackson—one of the most dangerous prisons in the Midwest—where in solitary confinement Dan looked in the mirror and with tears running down his face cried out in brokenness, "My God, this is all my own doing. What have I become?" It kept him safe in the institutional hell of men fighting men with death-dealing weapons made out of everything and anything. It protected him from gang involvement and even from violently acting out when he was threatened, accosted, or violated. In almost two decades in the system, Dan didn't catch one major ticket. Not even one. That's a miracle. That's the power of the love of God.

I watched the love of the Father heal the rage and hate and damage of Dan's lost childhood. He clung to that love when he was sent back into the system five times after first being eligible for parole. The Father's love kept us walking together all eighteen years of his sentence, through letters, visits, and phone calls—and even my little girls sending pictures they had drawn of Christmas trees, puppy dogs, and birthday cakes to, yeah, a violent sex offender. That love led him to Jesus in 1999 and finally released him from prison almost ten years later.

I will never, ever forget the day Dan first shared his story with Hope Community Church of Detroit, the group of Jesus' followers I am privileged to shepherd and the church that became his church because they wrote him, sent him money, and loved him when he had almost no one else. Dan closed out his talk that day with these words: "To my Hope family, I want to say that I understand if you don't want to be close to me. I understand if you don't trust me because I am a felon and I was a violent man and did some horrible things to human beings just like you. But I want you to know that if you do approach me these days, not only will I not hurt you, but I will more than likely throw my arms around your neck and kiss you on the cheek and whisper in your ear that I love you. Because of the power of the love of God, I am not the same man that I used to be. I am a new man. I am a new creation in Christ Jesus."

Just a few moments later, Dan stood at the front of the church with some other brothers and sisters, serving the Eucharist—the body and blood of Jesus—to all who were willing to get out of their seats and take a walk down the aisle to receive it. One of those who came that day was Dan's ex-wife Christine, a woman he had cheated on and abused. Two others walked right beside her—Dan and Christine's grown son and daughter, whom Dan had hurt and abandoned so many years ago. I watched as this wounded, shattered family took the body and blood of a loving Christ from the calloused hands of the husband and father who had damaged them so deeply. And I watched as God began to heal relationships so broken and human beings so emotionally and spiritually injured that any sane person would have said there was no way they'd ever be whole.

But for the power of love. A love that had begun to miraculously heal me. A love that would continue to heal Dan and is still healing his family.

Listen, we're about to embark on a hard road, you and I. A road through our emptiness and shame and woundedness. As you wrestle with your pain along the way—and even struggle with the difficulty of believing God loves you— remember Dan's story. Because no matter where you've been, what you've done, or what you've been through, you're heading toward a love that Jesus and his followers said was the power behind the covering and healing of all the sin and all the mess in all the world. A love that is powerful enough to heal . . . *you.*

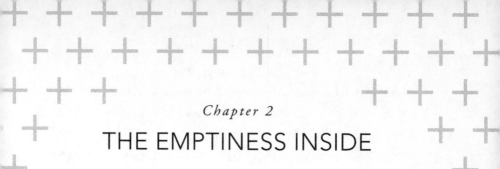

Chapter 2

THE EMPTINESS INSIDE

All the lonely people
Where do they all come from?
All the lonely people
Where do they all belong?
THE BEATLES, "ELEANOR RIGBY"

I bow my knees to the Father . . . that He would grant you . . . to know
the love of Christ . . . that you may be filled with all the fullness of God.
PAUL, EPHESIANS 3:14, 16, 19, NKJV

UNLIKE DAN, from childhood, Brian seemed to have it made. He was intelligent, athletic, and good-looking. Raised in Brazil as a missionary kid, he knew all the Christian stuff inside and out. He excelled at an academically rigorous Christian university in the States; married a sweet, intelligent, beautiful Christian girl with whom he had a few wonderful Christian kids; and worked hard and made a bunch of "God is blessing me" Christian money. He became a founding elder at one of the largest Christian churches in America and even had such a sensitive Christian conscience that he left suburban ease and led his family to urban Detroit to live a more deeply sacrificial Christian life.

Anyone who met Brian would have said, "This guy's the whole package. He's full, satisfied, and has what everyone else longs for." But do you want the truth? Brian was empty. Because even with all of his great Christian and societal whatevers, like Dan, he didn't have a clue that he was loved personally and passionately by God.

When I first met Brian, the emptiness was leaking out everywhere. Over lunch one day, I asked him, "So, Brian, what are you afraid of?" And maybe because of the love that was all over that conversation, Brian didn't blow me off or give me a Christian-ese response. Instead he began telling me about the business trip he had just returned from and the massage parlor he had stopped at on the way home and his years-long addiction to pornography and food. Out it came like an erupting volcano—everything that had been hidden for decades underneath the veneer of a missionary kid, church elder, happy family guy, and successful businessman. He was sick and tired of living a lie, of looking full but being empty and failing to fill up his emptiness even with the "right" stuff, like hard work and family and church. It was never enough.

He was depressed and losing his will to live. Long-term emptiness of spirit makes you want to die. Maybe that's why Paul cries out to God in one of his letters, "Please, Father, let people root deep in your love and the love of your Son so they can be filled with *your* fullness" (Ephesians 3:17-19, author's paraphrase). Maybe Paul was trying to say that if we don't know and experience the love that fills us, we live emptily—and it feels like we're *already* dead.

Brian's "living death" was all about the lie Satan has been telling each of us from the very beginning. In Genesis 3, Satan said to Adam and Eve, "That tree God said would kill you? Not true. In fact, it's the fruit of that very tree that will satisfy you and fill you up—and make you just like him" (verses 1-5, author's paraphrase). The ultimate meaning behind Satan's lie? "By keeping this good tree from you, God proves that he doesn't love you. He only loves himself."

God says, "I created you. I love you. Nothing will fill you except my love." And his enemy lies, saying, "Not so. He doesn't love you. And the only thing that will fill you is the very fruit of whatever he's keeping from you." If, like Adam and Eve, we believe this lie, we will inevitably move away from our God and move toward Satan's fruit, which has been deliciously flavored by the forces of darkness for our particular taste. But Satan's fruit never satisfies. Never, ever. A successful German businessman once came to me and said, with quivering lip, "After hearing you speak about the power of the love of God to fill our hearts, I finally realize that I have everything—but I have nothing."

If we believe this age-old satanic lie that God doesn't love us and that something outside of his love can satisfy our spirits, we will spend every day of our lives gorging ourselves on fruit that will never fill us. The fruit is poison. From the very first bite, we begin to waste away. Satan hates our guts and lies to us because he wants us dead. He's not playing. Do we get that?

A few summers ago I was sitting in my office when I

heard gunshots. I ran out the door and down the street just in time to see a young man fall into a gutter. Moments earlier he had been shot in the lot across from the church—the same lot where all our people park on Sunday mornings. Later I heard that the shooting was about a drug deal gone bad. Two guys shot this young man in the face. As I looked at his body, his head on the curb, torso in the street, arms flopped awkwardly at his side, I thought, *Man, he doesn't hardly look grown—just a kid, really.* And then the passionately angry thought, *Satan, you just killed a boy.* As I stood there, three feet from his body, I started weeping for this young man who was in very real ways my brother. I cried tears of grief and rage against a spiritual enemy I would have strangled on the spot if I could.

I stood there on the street with others from the neighborhood, our arms around one another, our brother's body at our feet. We prayed and shouted out loud at God and begged for mercy. I can remember saying, "Father, you love this young man. You wanted to fill him up with your love for him as your son. But somehow, he didn't get it, and now he's gone." This precious son of God believed the lie of Satan, who hated his guts and wanted him dead, who told him the fruit was sweet and would satisfy. So he bit into the fruit and kept on eating—and now he *was* dead.

This kind of story is so graphic and bloody that it just might convince us for a minute that Satan really isn't playing. That he really does want us dead. But my fear is we could quickly forget. We might say, "Yeah, that's how it is for folks in rough neighborhoods or people who are desperate enough to mess with guns and drugs." But this whole "believe the lie and you die" truth is not about being urban or suburban; or being black, white, Asian, or Latino; or being rich or broke. It's about all of us being human. The emptiness inside of us has to be filled, and we all wrestle with the lie that it can be filled with anything but the love of God.

The lie can take on many forms, and the enemy can use the lie in many different ways to kill us. The lie can be that drugs and a fistful of cash will fix everything, and like this boy, death can come from a gunshot wound to the face. But the lie can also be that good stuff like family and career and soccer leagues and church and accomplishment can fill up our lives—and the death is a slow, poisonous rot from the inside out. Satan doesn't need drugs and gunshots to the face. He loves to use even the cancerous good stuff to kill us.

Brian and I had success and achievement—a bold, sweet fruit cocktail that left each of us so empty that Brian moved toward pornography and I became a rage addict. Both of us almost killed our marriages and eventually thought about killing ourselves. Dead is dead. And when we believe the lie that God doesn't love us and that his love cannot fill us, no matter the version of that lie—it always, always leads us to our death.

But is there an alternative? If even the best that life has to offer doesn't completely fill us, then is there any real possibility of being filled? There absolutely is. We can be filled with the love of a God who calls himself our Father and our Lover and who loves us as if we are his only love. As my young brother fell that day in the street, I pray he heard what I know the Father was whispering in his ear: "I love you, son. I'm here. I've got you. And I promise you, I'm never letting you go." That's exactly what God whispered to Brian that day at lunch. There's something about hitting bottom and being scary honest about our emptiness that gets us to the place of choosing to listen. So for the first time in all his forty-five religious years on the planet, over pancakes and coffee, Brian began to hear God say, "Son, I am your Father, and I love you so much. And no matter what, I will love you forever." And when this truth finally hit Brian's empty spirit, a filling, satisfying, life-changing love affair was born.

Over the last six years, the real Brian—beloved, healing son of God—has finally emerged. Addiction to pornography all but gone, sent back to hell where it came from—because of the strong love of God. Gut-level honesty with his wife and true intimacy for the first time ever—because of the strong love of God. A new openness and mutual respect with his grown children—because of the strong love of God. A deep and courageous transparency—because of the strong love of God.

Brian now leads a small group of young men, and every week he brings the brothers back to, "Hey, do you know—*really know*—that God loves you?" One of his guys, a brilliant young brother named Sam, was a walking cavern a few years ago—deeply depressed, hopelessly addicted to porn, and watching his marriage die. The love of God began to pour out of Brian into Sam, and now Sam is starting to believe that God just might love him, too. The strong love of God is slowly but surely bringing Sam's heart and his marriage back to life. Just like Brian's. Just like mine. Because that's what the Father's love always, always does. It fills up our emptiness. It brings us back to life. Every time.

Chapter 3

JUST A KID

Something happened to us a long time ago. It happened more than once. It hurt us. We protected ourselves the only way we knew how. We are still protecting ourselves. It isn't working anymore.
JOHN AND LINDA FRIEL, *Adult Children*

Teach your kids night and day about the love of God the Father, who loves them unconditionally and forever.
DEUTERONOMY 6:4-9, 7:6-8, AUTHOR'S PARAPHRASE

ARE PEOPLE BORN EMPTY—or does that emptiness creep in over a lifetime?

I met Kennell when I first came to the Jefferson-Chalmers neighborhood of Detroit in 2006. Eighteen years old, tall, good-looking, articulate, with a winsome smile when he felt free enough to wear it, Kennell walked the neighborhood with shoulders bent, head bowed, and an oversized sweatshirt draped over his head and body. Everything about his posture said, *Don't mess with me, and I won't mess with you.* One day, of course, I approached him anyway.

You've got to understand—I didn't wake up that morning with a plan to reach out to Kennell Delbridge. But when I saw him that particular afternoon, I could feel his pain and emptiness. Looking at Kennell was like looking at myself in the mirror fifteen years earlier.

I can't remember if he was standing on the street corner by the church where some of the young men hung out, talking and joking and sharing a smoke or a joint, or on the church porch before a Wednesday pizza, job-training, Bible study event that regularly drew young men and women from the community (mostly for the pizza). But one day I went up to Kennell, reached out my hand, drew him close, hugged him, and then looked him in the eye and said, "Hey, man, my name's Kevin. You wanna hang out sometime?" Our relationship was birthed at that moment, and slowly, over the next several years, he began to tell me about a life that from the very beginning had known very little love.

Kennell's mom was a crack addict. These days, she is in recovery and loves God and works hard to love all of her children and grandchildren well. But early on, Kennell and his brothers were farmed out to foster parents. His mom got clean and regained custody of him when Kennell was ten years old, but much damage had already been done. A few years later, Kennell's dad got into an altercation with a family member, threw lighter fluid on the guy's body, and lit him on fire. When Kennell and I met, his father was still serving an eight-year sentence in the Michigan correctional system. He has since gotten out and seems to simply be trying to find his way, like the rest of us. But again, in Kennell's life, much damage had already been done.

As I got to know Kennell, I discovered he was depressed and using anything he could find—weed or cards or sex or whatever—to fill the emptiness in his spirit. He had already been to jail a few times and didn't want to go back. But nothing in his life motivated him except music that gave expression to his pain. "Pastor," Kennell told me one day, "I feel like there's a hopeless dome over my head and around my life, and honestly, I don't think there's any way out."

What happened to make a bright, athletic, tender young man think that his life was not even worth living? Sure, a whole lot of mess got downloaded into Kennell at a young age. But one thing was more wounding and death-dealing than anything else: Kennell flat-out didn't get enough love.

This isn't rocket science. Kids come out of the womb looking for someone to tell them who they are, what life is about, what matters—and if *they* matter. Parents are supposed to pour into their children the heart-filling reality that they are loved. In fact, the pledge of allegiance of Judaism—the Shema (Deuteronomy 6:4-9), recited twice a day in the Israeli community for generations—is in part, the command for parents to know not only the commands but *the love* of the one true God in their own hearts . . . and then to pass on those commands—saturated in that love— to their kids. If children are well loved, they tend to live loving, giving, hope-filled, relationally healthy lives. But if abuse or abandonment or even benign neglect is their primary experience, they tend to grow up empty, the voices inside their heads shouting *you'll never be enough*. Instead of becoming givers—filled with love—these children grow up to be takers, sucking the life out of everything and everyone around them because in their emptiness they have very little to give.

Parental love is supposed to be a living, breathing portrait of a God who calls himself Father and who loves each of his kids no matter what. No parental love? Weak parental love? Parents who unintentionally drip their own emptiness and baggage into their children's lives? Those kids are going to have a hard time believing God gives half a care about their lives, because in the midst of their emptiness a loud satanic voice shouts, "God doesn't love you! Just like your parents don't love you. He never has. Never will."

This pain is in so many people's stories.

I think about Melissa, a Michigan State coed raised in suburban Hartland, Michigan. Her mom and dad split up when she was a little girl—and by age thirteen, living with her mother, she naturally began to wonder why her daddy didn't pursue her more frequently or passionately. He said it was because she looked too much like her mom. Seeing her caused him too much pain. She told me this story one Sunday afternoon as I visited her in the women's prison in Ypsilanti, Michigan, where we sat once a month for several hours in the break room, eating fake cheese burritos and jalapeño Doritos and candy bars and drinking Diet Coke. At the age of twenty-one, Melissa was sent to prison for the death of one of her closest friends. He'd been riding in the passenger seat one night when Melissa, intoxicated and behind the wheel, drove up an exit ramp, entered the expressway going the wrong way, and hit two cars head-on.

"When did your drinking start?" I asked her that Sunday afternoon.

"A few years after my dad said he didn't want to see me because I looked too much like my mother," she said.

Of course.

To be sure, Melissa knows she made her own choices over the years. She's not trying to blame her dad for her decisions. But the reality is, when kids don't get the love they need, they act out because they are just as desperate as grown folks to fill up the vacuum inside.

Remember, we really do have a spiritual enemy, and he really is trying to kill us. And his main strategy is simply to convince us that we're dirt, that we're not enough, that we're losers—that we're unloved. And what better place to start than in the home, through parents who are supposed to be the main vehicle of that love to tender and impressionable children? Parents who all too often, tragically, don't know anything of that love themselves.

The enemy is such a lying chameleon that sometimes the lack of love in a home isn't all that obvious. A few years ago, I sat with Nathan, the young leader of a campus ministry, who proudly shared with me, "I never *feel* the love of God as my Father—but it doesn't matter. I know he loves me because the Bible says it's true. And that's all I need."

I said to him, "Son, if I was your earthly father and you told me you had never experienced love from me, but you somehow knew it in your head because I wrote it to you one time in a birthday card—it would break my heart. You know why? Because as a dad I would know that it isn't enough to have words about my father love in your head. The words alone will never sustain you. They will never give you life. It is only in the *experience* of my love as a dad that you will flourish and grow, and that's all a dad wants for his little boy—to live free, saturated in the rock-solid foundation of his father love. Nathan, if I feel this way about you as an earthly father, how much more do you think your heavenly Father wants you to know his love—not just from a holy book, but deep in your heart?"

For a long, long moment, Nathan was dead silent. And when he replied, his voice was filled with something I'll never forget. I can only describe it as longing. "Kevin," he said, "would it be all right if I sent you an e-mail?"

A couple of weeks later, we began an online dialogue, and after a few questions about his relationship with his parents over the years, out it came.

Dad and Mom didn't really tell me they loved me that often. They weren't really very demonstrative or warm. They believed in God, and they were good people, but they were not very good at expressing their love to me as a son. I guess I thought that's just how it was, how it had to be—even with God.

The lack of love in the life of a child—overt or subtle, but always deadly.

So is there any hope? For Kennell or Melissa or Nathan or me . . . or you? I mean, if your parents intentionally or unintentionally screw it all up, and you grow up without a clue that God loves you, and your emptiness is bleeding out over every relationship in your life—is there a way out? A way to be healed? A way to be filled?

Absolutely. The antidote to un-love is simply to be loved. Again, like Peter, one of Jesus' main followers, said, "Above everything else, love one another with deep passion, for that kind of love will cover, heal, and redeem a whole lot of sin" (1 Peter 4:8, author's paraphrase). The wound of being unloved cries out for the healing experience of being loved.

I once spoke to a group of high school girls, many of them orphaned or raised in single-parent homes, about the deep love of God the Father for his daughters. I shared over and over through Scripture and stories that the Father loved them and delighted in them and that he held each of them in the palms of his mighty, loving hands. They listened intently. Afterward, one of the young women came up to me, slipped her hand into mine, looked up at me, and asked, "Will you be my father?" She didn't even know me. But she longed to be healed by being loved. Because the healing answer to the wound of un-love is always, always to be loved.

Nathan told me recently that as his parents have deepened their love relationship with Jesus, they've grown in the way they give away love and affection. And not surprisingly, the love they have always had for Nathan and are now learning to express to him is helping to heal Nathan's ability to experience the love of the Father. Of course. Because authentic, felt love always heals the wounds of feeling unloved.

In the same way, for the last nine years, I have loved Kennell as if he were my son. Not because I have to or feel like it is my duty—Kennell would sense that kind of fake affection a mile away, and love that isn't authentic isn't healing. It would only add to his feeling that in and of himself, he isn't worthy of love. The reason I show Kennell love is because I truly love him. I've got a God who loves me as a son, and so I love Kennell as if he were my son. It's that simple—but also that profound. You can't love anyone well without knowing God's love. And when you know God's love, you can't stop loving those around you.

So I love Kennell. I love him by calling him and texting him and telling him over and over that I love him. I pray with him, pray over him, and pray for him. I have visited him in jail. We have worked side by side on projects at the church and in the neighborhood. We've talked both on the phone and for hours sitting in my car. I've helped him when he was short of cash, not because I'm a pastor but because that's how I would love him if he were my son. I married him to his childhood sweetheart, and I counseled them during their struggle, and now I'm walking with him through his tragic divorce. I love him by getting in his face once in a while when he's done something stupid, but I have earned that right because he knows I love him. When he has a question or a need, he knows he can call me. He knows I'm thinking about him constantly because that's what love does. And Kennell knows that no matter what, my love isn't going away.

Because of love, Kennell is healing. I'd like to tell you that his healing has been quick and that the results are perfect. I'd like to tell you he has healed so much that he has given his life to be a missionary in Tibet or that he walks around Detroit all day every day sharing Jesus with people and living off of manna from heaven. But that wouldn't be true. Kennell is healing, but like all of us, he still struggles. And sometimes his healing seems painfully slow, even and maybe especially to himself. But he has hope again. He has dignity and personhood for the first time ever. He is enrolled in college and looking hard—real hard—for a job that can sustain him and enable him to help others who have no hope. Because as love heals us, it compels us to love others. Kennell is softer, kinder, and more deeply sensitive to the pain around him than he has ever been. He wants to help his mom, who works a couple of jobs; and his dad, who is a mechanic; and his sister, who is a single mom; and two of his brothers, who are in prison.

A few Sundays ago after church, Kennell hugged me and told me he loved me. And he said something to me he had never, ever said before: "Pastor, I love you—*very, very much.*" That might not seem like a big deal to anyone else. But for some reason, in that moment, his words seemed to me to be shouting, "You can't have me, Satan. You hit me with your best shot when I was just a little boy, but the love of God has rescued me and is healing me, and now I'm healing others. And I don't just have love—I've got *much* love."

And Melissa? Like Kennell—and so many of the rest of us—she still struggles with guilt and shame at times. She knows that she will always live with deep, deep regret over the part she played in the loss of her friend. But love is healing her, too. Her mom's love. The love of her believing friends in the campus ministry at Michigan State, where she first heard about a man named Jesus who loved her so much that he died for her. The love of her brothers and sisters in her church, where they don't just talk love, they *actually* love. And she is being healed by the love of a young man named Phil who became her husband on December 27, 2013. She's no longer empty, but full.

All this love is healing Melissa . . . and Kennell and Nathan and Dan and Brian and me . . . and I'm telling you, if it can heal us, it can heal anyone. It can even heal you. Because it really is true that love covers, heals, and redeems a whole lot of sin—even the devastation of being unloved when you were just a kid.

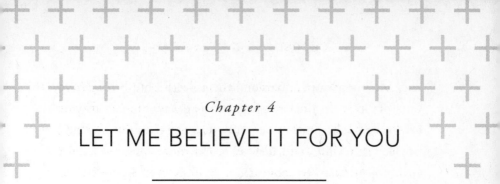

Chapter 4

LET ME BELIEVE IT FOR YOU

The great turning point in your life comes not when you
realize that you love God but when you realize and fully
accept the fact that God loves you unconditionally.
ANTHONY DE MELLO, *Sadhana, A Way to God*

This is the most profound spiritual truth I know: that even when
we're most sure that love can't conquer all, it seems to anyway.
ANNE LAMOTT, *Traveling Mercies*

AT THE END of *The Wizard of Oz*, the Wizard gives the
Scarecrow his diploma, the Tin Man his "heart," and the
Cowardly Lion his medal for courage. And then the Scarecrow
gets in the Wizard's face and says, "Hey, what about Dorothy?"
I always get tears in my eyes when I hear Dorothy reply: "Oh,
I don't think there's anything in that black bag for me."

A few weeks after my initial exhilaration of connecting with
the love of God in *The Ragamuffin Gospel* and believing that it
really was true—he loves *me*!—I hit a wall. Once again, I began
to believe that there was nothing in God's bag of love for me—
that he truly loved everyone else in the world—but probably
not shame-based, rageaholic, inadequate husband and father

me. My initial hopefulness and the powerful but brief experience of God's personal love began to give way to a dark despair.

I called a therapist to help me along the path to some kind of deeper healing, and it was a good move—maybe even a loving-God inspired move. Because early on in our relationship, I turned to the counselor, Gary, and asked him, "Do you really think that I will ever deeply know—in any kind of sustainable way—that God truly loves me?"

I will never forget his reply: "Yes, Kevin. I've been where you are, and by God's grace, I don't live there any longer. I promise. You *will* know the love of God in a deep and sustainable way. And until you can believe that for yourself—let me believe it for you."

Gary's life-saving words are the reason that I want to tell you about my friend Samson. Because I know that some of you are already saying, "I get it. And I get that's it's true for all these people you've been talking about. But I really don't think there's anything in that bag of love . . . for me."

I hear you. Remember, I've lived it. So for those of you who can't help thinking that God loves everyone else but you, I want to tell Samson's story. Because if there ever was a guy I thought might be too far gone for the love of God to touch or to heal—besides myself—it was Samson. And when you hear Samson's story, I think you might also hear Samson's voice saying to your broken heart, "You're going to be all right. You *are* going to know the deep love of God. I promise. And until you can believe that for yourself, let me, Samson Wright, believe it for you."

Samson is thirty years old and lives in a federal peniten-tiary, where he's serving a fifteen-year sentence for allegedly committing a crime I can't talk about much because there are appeals in process. But I met him in late 2005 when a young ex-con named KD brought Samson to the church one afternoon. KD was an extremely wounded young man who had done a whole lot of really bad stuff and served a whole lot of time and turned out to be a chronic liar. So eventually after a couple of years of trying to live life alongside him, I sadly watched KD walk away. I truly wish I knew where he was today so we could try again. But I don't. Samson, on the other hand, stuck around. We started hanging out, and slowly but surely he began to tell me about his life.

No father, and an abusive—real abusive—mother. She was a religious woman—actually a member of a popular, modern-day religious cult—but nevertheless, a hater. And let's just say that under her watch, Samson grew up a mega-hurt kid. Believe me when I tell you that if half of what Samson shared with me about his childhood is true, the abuse was deep and pervasive. You know the saying "Hurt people hurt people"? That was the case with Samson. When we met he hadn't yet been to prison, but he had been in the Wayne County Jail seven times for various things—drugs and fighting and thug-ging and a scam or two. But what concerned me was Samson was really big, really strong, and really, really angry. Samson was filled with rage at a world that had only given him pain. I remember thinking that it was only a matter of time before this dude was going to wind up killing or being killed.

I don't remember the first time I witnessed Samson's rage. But I do remember the time I walked with—no, chased— Samson all over our neighborhood as he waved his huge arms and shouted expletives at the top of his lungs about someone who had hurt him that day. I'm talking about two solid hours of Samson raging and me trying to talk him down and actually being pretty scared that he might turn on me until finally I said, "Son, I get your anger because you know I've struggled with it all my life. I ain't judgin' you now, but either you begin to calm down—or I love you enough to call the cops to keep you from doing something that will land you in prison for the rest of your life." Miraculously, he didn't deck me. Instead, he decided to chill.

I also remember the time Samson came to the church and confessed he had just shot a guy he worked with. In the butt, no less. Then he told us the brother he shot was now in the hospital, and he asked if we could help him get some clothes and some food and magazines together so he could go visit him and see how he was doing. Yeah, you got it—Samson wanted to go make a pastoral call on the guy he just shot.

Because you see, Samson had this other side to him. Underneath the pain and rage was this soft, giving, grizzly teddy bear of a human being—the kind of guy who could be quick with a joke, a smile, and an encouraging word and would always be the first to volunteer to stay overnight the entire week if necessary when the church hosted forty homeless folks from one of Detroit's traveling shelters.

Samson had been homeless himself at times, staying here

and there in the darkest places in our city. For a while he stayed with a grandmother he really cared for. She was a nice lady, but she was really, really sick. We took her food and medicine and prayed with her and hugged her a lot. But I've got to tell you, I've seen better living conditions in the third world. The filth and smell and hopeless atmosphere were stifling. There was a boatload of hurting human beings packed into the home. And for a while Samson slept in a back section of this house—I can't say "room" because only a curtain made out of an old sheet separated his space from the rest of the human chaos. So even when Samson wasn't homeless, he lived in mess that was sometimes almost subhuman—which I think reflected the emptiness, pain, chaos, and, of course, rage that Samson felt in his heart.

For the most part, Samson walked alone. He didn't trust anyone and figured he was way better off going solo—even if unloved. That is until he started hanging out with the family of wounded healers at Hope Community Church and some folks began to love him in a way he had never been loved before. I'll never forget the first night I saw the love of God break through the layers of Samson's broken heart.

It was Thanksgiving Eve 2005. We had a service at the church where folks could write down their wounds; walk to the front of the church; and, hoping for some kind of healing, symbolically nail their pain-laden piece of paper to a huge wooden cross lying on the altar. That evening, Pam, a platinum blonde, big-hair, believing sister from the suburbs, was sitting close to Samson. And the God of love must

have spoken to her—because Samson could be an impos-
ing, frightening presence, but Pam moved closer and closer
to him, unafraid. Love always seems to overcome fear. She
began talking quietly with Samson about her own wounds,
his wounds, and the healing offered to them both by Jesus
Christ. I watched her walk with Samson to the front of
the church, where she helped him take his crumpled list of
bloody, abusive childhood memories and experiences—story
after story of how the enemy had tried to kill his spirit and
life—and pound it, with great passion and, yes, rage into a
cross symbolizing the healing love of Christ.

I mention that she was a sister from the suburbs only to
say that in order to help one another heal and begin to know
the love of God, we don't need to have much in common
except our humanity and pain and a willingness to share that
pain with Jesus. That night God gave Pam love for Samson
when he was in a very vulnerable place, and the love she
shared began to heal him—and I think his openness and
vulnerability helped heal her and her wounds as well.

In almost eight years of relationship, Samson and I had
many Wendy's lunches and Big Boy dinners and countless
deep talks over burgers and fries. Samson didn't have wheels,
and the public transportation in Detroit stinks, so we did
some of our best connecting in my dark green '99 Dodge
Durango. Along the way, I truly began feeling toward him
like I feel toward Kennell—like a father feels toward a son.
We would argue and disagree, and sometimes I wouldn't see
him for a while. But I really love Samson, and I think he

loves me. And I really think our love for each other—a love that comes from God—has helped heal Samson and, frankly, continues to heal us both.

One of my favorite memories in thirty-two years of being a pastor is baptizing Samson on Thanksgiving Sunday 2006. I know for sure it was that day because Samson gave me his dated baptismal certificate to keep for him. He told me that just in case he ever needed it, he wanted to be sure he knew where it was. I wouldn't trade that piece of paper for anything.

And today Samson is in prison. For real. Healing usually isn't a straight line from the pain to some kind of wholeness. Mine hasn't been, and Samson's hasn't been either. In the years after his baptism, he was in and out of church, in and out of Bible studies, and in and out of relationship with various folks in the Hope Community. He had been diagnosed as bipolar and didn't take his meds much because they made him feel zoned out and subhuman, so it was sometimes difficult for him to sit still. Even when Samson came to church, he would often stand at the door as security or stand at the back—always watching and intently listening but rarely sitting down. And he was still hypersensitive and could get deeply offended over even innocent looks or comments. When that happened, Samson was either going to confront you in rage or pull back. More and more in the last six or seven years, he just pulled back.

But in his own way, Samson stayed connected. Even when he didn't show up for a church service for weeks on end, he would still regularly come to the building on a weekday to talk to me or one of the others who loved him. And during this time of simple, consistent, loving connection—the first that Samson had ever known in his life—something powerful was happening inside his wounded heart and spirit. Samson Wright, who for most of his life had walked alone, was being healed by the heart of a loving God.

In the Western church, we've gotten it into our heads that there's one way to heal and grow, and that's primarily through a transfer of information, through a Bible study or a sermon. But what if the wounds are so deep that the truth can't be received? Or to use neurobiological categories, what if the wounded right brain—where we experience our feelings and engage in relationship—can't receive what the left brain can obviously understand? It's one thing to have "God loves you and has a wonderful plan for your life" preached at you and to say, "Yeah, I can intellectually understand those concepts." But it is quite another to really start to "get it" deep within your heart and spirit, in the core places of your being, to be able to say, "I'm starting to experience his love that is high and wide and deep and long, and it is literally filling me up."

How did the criminal dying next to Jesus two thousand years ago "get it"? He was the last person who should have ever "gotten it." You didn't get nailed to a Roman cross for purse-snatching, so whether he was a murderer, rapist, or insurrectionist, in the eyes of Roman society, this guy was done. Gone. No hope. Needed to die. So what happened that changed him? There was no time and no emotional room in the midst of the torture for a theological lecture. Jesus didn't instruct him on the Ten Commandments or even ask him if he was ready to amend his life. But as Jesus turned toward the man, something happened. The man's brokenness began to heal. The rock-hard, bitter, forsaken, beyond-hope human being who had mocked Jesus just moments before got soft— and chose to believe. Could it be that he was healed by the power of Jesus' love, a love that he felt and sensed beyond any words or theology, even while Jesus was dying? Just like "beyond hope" me and "beyond hope" Samson Wright?

Samson is a really smart guy, and early on he heard the Scripture at Hope Community in sermons and Bible studies and sort of "got it"—intellectually. But he was so wounded that for a while he just couldn't "get it" deep within his spirit. And yet over eight years' time, the love of Jesus Christ, often through his wounded-healer brothers and sisters, began to slowly and surely bring the dead little boy inside Samson back to absolute life. Today Samson, in prison no less, is finally beginning to truly and deeply know that he matters and has purpose and that there is a God who is his Father who loves him like a true son.

Though I always knew God loved Samson, I did think Samson might be the guy who was too wounded and too broken for the love of the Father to touch and heal. But today I can tell you that the strong love of the Father *is* healing him. It is that same strong love that is waiting to heal you—even if you've been convinced by the enemy, "There's nothing in that bag of love for me."

Let me share an astounding note with you that I received from Samson a few months back, handwritten from his prison cell. I've recorded it exactly as he wrote it so you can feel his heart:

Dear Pastor,

How are you doing find I hope. I got your letter. For the frist time in life that I frounded price with myself. I learned a lot from you pastor you just don't know how it make's me feel now. Its my honour to call you Pastor, friend and my father in Christ. I remember when I frist came to the church with KD and I met you and Sue for the frist time. And we had a bound with each other from that point. I met your family and you met some of my family. We like two pea's in the pot my friend. I have a job to finnish and it's right by your side pastor. All this was a wake up call for me telling me to chill out. I know its been a long time since I was at the church and y'all still have my back to this day and it's a blessing to still have y'all in my corner. I know sometime I mite ask you for something its only because I look at you like family. Sometimes I ask myself if I can go back in time what would I do. I say to my self nothing sometime we have to learn from are mistakes.

Look now when I look at the sky I see something their that God wants me to do. All I used to see is darkness now I see the light. Now I putting trust in God

*something I never did before. I believe in God now and
everything you had said about Jesus died for my sins for
me. You is a god fearing man like I want to do now. I
use to say that I did not have anything to live for and
life was a joke. If I had to give you award it wood be
my trust, my heart and my friendship with a hole lot
of love . . .*

Love, Samson

Raging hater—too wounded and too far gone to ever
truly understand, to ever be healed. Now a son of God filled
with a "hole lot of love." Miracle.

And if some of you are saying, "Hey, guys in prison will
say anything to get some help on the outside," check this out.
A little while ago, some of our Sunday School kids sent cards
to our prisoners. A little girl named Evelyn wrote to Samson.
And Samson wrote back:

Dear Evelyn,

*Thanks for the card it was sweet. I did like the card you
sent me. I pray every day asking God to help and guide
me through this. Hey I bet you didn't know sometimes I
teach the Bible in here. I talk about God every day. From
a friend to a friend this is my prayer to God for you.*

*Dear Lord thanks for sending me a little friend
Evelyn. She have a lot to know about you so do I. Guide*

her throw life as she grow up. Sometime she mite not understand everything with your help father God she will. Let her know you have a place for her and me in your kingdom. Protect her when she need help father God. Let her know as long as she have her family and the church an also you God that everything will be all right. In your son Jesus name amen.

From a friend to a friend,
Samson

Some letters just cannot lie.

Wounded, doubting son or daughter of God, can you hear Samson calling out to you? Can you hear him saying, "Listen to me. I used to doubt too. I didn't think God could ever love someone like me. Or that I would ever truly get it. But he does love me, and today I *know* that he loves me. I am getting full. I have reason to live, even in prison. And I'm telling you, the same is going to be true for you. And until you can believe it for yourself, let me, Samson Wright, believe it for you."

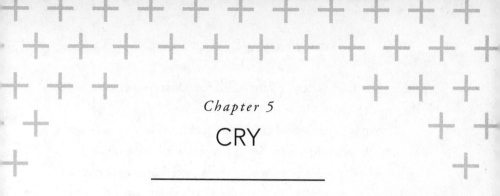

Chapter 5

CRY

There is no sorrow that God cannot heal . . .
Jesus the Lord of the lonely inside
MICHAEL KELLY BLANCHARD,
"JESUS, LORD OF THE LONELY INSIDE"

Weeping may endure for a night, but joy comes in the morning.
PSALM 30:5, NKJV

IT WOULD BE great if we believed it when someone told us, "Hey, God loves you." Then that love would land in our hearts and heal us and fill us up—and we could spend the rest of our lives being loved and loving everyone and everything around us. If only we could hear the voice of God calling us his beloved. Jesus heard it when he was baptized by his cousin John. The voice of God shouted, "You are My beloved Son, in whom I am well pleased" (Mark 1:11, NKJV). If we could just hear that voice and feel that love, we would absolutely be healed. But that voice is the most difficult voice to hear. Why? Well, of course—because of all the other voices.

"I've never been nothin' but a crackhead ho." That's what Sophia Wyatt said when she sat down with me one night to tell me her story. That's what she believed about herself for more than twenty years. Because that's what the voices told her. Like the voice of her wife-beating, womanizing father, who drank away all his money and left the family with nothing but "neck bone and black-eyed peas" most nights. Or the voices of the various pimps and a multitude of johns who used her until all she could hear was, "I am trash. I must be trash—why else would all these men treat me like trash?"

Many of us have these same kinds of voices whispering and some days shouting at us: "You'll never be enough. Who do you think you're fooling? Don't you get it? You're nothing." The voice might be the specter of our dad or mom, a grandparent, teacher, pastor or coach, a former boss or best friend, or even our entire seventh-grade class. Sometimes it's not even an actual voice but the lack of a voice. Like the dad who might be a decent human being but never tells his daughter that she is beautiful or rarely tells his son that he is proud of him. Never hearing these words from a parent says clearly to a child, "You're not worth the effort it takes my heart to tell you I love you."

For many of us, these shaming voices or the pain of their rejection speaks so loudly that most days we simply cannot hear the voice of our God calling us His beloved.

So, do the voices ever, ever stop?

That's what Sophia wailed out of the deepest parts of her heart one Sunday morning when she stood up in church—in the middle of the sermon—and cried out, "O God, when is this going to stop hurting? I can't sleep. I can't eat. Pastor Butcher, when, when, when will the voices go away?"

I didn't know it then, but I know it now—that morning Sophia started her journey to deeper healing, to quieting and stilling the shaming voices of her past. Because that morning she started to grieve, to lament, crying out her deep pain to God in the safe presence of some folks who love her unconditionally. Sophia began to give voice to her pain, which set her on the pathway to healing.

Research tells us that "it is difficult to give language to pain, that pain is language shattering" but that if we want to heal, "we need to find language to express that pain."[2] Maybe this is why the earliest communities of Jesus followers were instructed to "weep with those who weep" (Romans 12:15, ESV) and why one of the earmarks of their intimate fellowship was that "if one member suffers, all the members suffer with it" (1 Corinthians 12:26, NASB). Maybe ancient believers knew what twenty-first-century Western believers sometimes seem to have forgotten—that grieving leads to healing. It is true not only that "weeping endures for the night and joy comes in the morning" (Psalm 55:22, author's paraphrase) but also that weeping literally leads to and creates space for the joy we all so desperately want to experience. When you see someone who seems to be shut down and struggling to experience the highs of life, it may be because they have not yet dealt with their wounds and pain. Hard things must be felt, grieved, and released in order to open up that part of the heart that feels joy. When we allow ourselves to grieve the wounding people and experiences in our lives, the screaming voices start to recede into the background. And slowly but surely we begin to hear the joyful voice of our God whispering, "I love you. I really, really love you."

In days gone by, industrial site cleanup experts tried to deal with toxic waste by putting dangerous chemicals and materials in steel drums and burying them deep beneath the surface of the ground. That was fine until twenty or thirty years down the road when the drums began to leak and spilled the deadly waste into the ground water, poisoning everyone and everything within its reach. The same is true for our pain. We might be able to store it away or hide it in a secret place in our hearts for a while. But eventually our hearts begin to leak, and our un-grieved pain and loss spills out into our lives and relationships, poisoning everyone and everything that matters to us. And that pain continues to poison us—and the shaming voices attached to the pain continue to shout—until the wound is grieved, lamented, and released into the hands of a caring, healing God.

Unfortunately, the church of Jesus—the same Jesus who wept all over the Gospels and who is called "man of sorrows, acquainted with bitterest grief" by the prophets (Isaiah 53:3, TLB)—seems uncomfortable with grief. Especially the middle-class, twenty-first-century Western church. We don't seem to know what to do with pain. Either it doesn't fit our theology, or it makes us feel emotionally awkward, or maybe we're simply afraid. Instead of being present to those who are hurting so they can grieve and eventually experience the love of the Father, we tend to "farm out" the folks who hurt too long or too loud.

One researcher noted the differences between ancient Jewish culture and church culture today—that Israelite priests were ready and willing to help the community process their pain and adversity, while the modern church, mimicking the larger death-denying culture, tends to suppress grief: "In fact, we are a culture which encourages individual therapy as a substitute for communal expressions of grief."[3]

Could it be that one main reason so many Jesus followers don't experience the deep love of God is because his church refuses to create space for grieving the very pain that keeps them from hearing his voice?

Some Christian types will say, "Hey, there are folks going to hell out there. We don't have time to grieve. We need to 'get over' our pain and get to the business of saving souls." Listen—dogs are meant to get over things. I can ignore my dog, Sadie, for twenty-four hours, and the next day she's right back sitting at my feet, waiting for some love. She gets over stuff because that's what dogs do. Humans, on the other hand, aren't meant to get over things. Humans are meant to grieve. We're created in the image of a God who loves and who calls us to love. We grieve because we love. The greater the love, the greater the loss, and the greater the need to grieve our way to joy.

Sophia Wyatt had much to grieve. Divorced with two children by the age of eighteen, Sophia went to work at a "high class" restaurant.

"I was a telephone answerer, then a hostess," she told me. "I dressed up every day and went to Winkleman's every day. Then I started going with the manager, and one night he said, 'Let's try some crack.' We started getting high every Friday. Then one time another girl said, 'You're wasting it like that—get a pipe and use it like *this*.' And that was it. From that time on, everybody wanted a piece of me."

Within two years Sophia quit the restaurant and started dancing topless at a club. "The money was good," she said. "I started doing parties. I could always get high. The dope boys loved to keep me high, so I guess I was fun. I looked good, ya know? I was manipulative. I could talk anybody out of anything—even the women." Soon the high became everything. Sophia quit the topless job and started prostituting herself on the street. She moved into a house with a few girls and got a pimp who gave them all the drugs they wanted.

And suddenly, that whole "Satan really is trying to kill us thing" kicked in and life got seriously dangerous. One day Sophia got high and was walking up Grand River on the Westside of Detroit when two guys pulled up in a car and said, "You want a ride?" When she said no, one of the guys pulled out a gun, trying to get her in the backseat. But a drunk guy standing nearby yelled out, "Leave her alone!" She took off running while the guys from the car started beating the drunk. Then what she thought was another car pulled up, and someone inside said, "Are you okay? I'll give you a lift." She got in and then realized it was the same guy and same car as before. As she threw herself out the car door onto the cement, the guy with the gun grabbed her ponytail. Thank God the hair was fake, Sophia told me. It came off in his hand. She was that close to being dead.

Another time in those early days of hooking, Sophia was on Chene and Gratiot and got into a truck with a guy who slashed her with a blade across her face so fast she didn't even see it coming. She fought and got away—and still went to get high later. She didn't go to the hospital until 10:00 p.m. that night. It took sixty-five stitches to sew up her cheek.

A few years down the road, one of her "boyfriends" pointed to her scar and said, "I should kick you out. There ain't gonna be no one who wants to take care of you because you're so ugly." When Sophia recounted this story to me, I really couldn't tell what hurt her worse—the deep, long, unsightly scar on the right side of her face or the voice of the boyfriend who reminded her of how she already felt inside.

Finally came the night that made Sophia say, "Anybody would have thought that enough was enough." She was dancing, tricking, and getting high at a party when she had a seizure from the drugs.

"My mother said she was watching the news, and I flashed across the screen," Sophia told me. "They were saying they found me in a dumpster, almost dead. When I seizured and fell out, apparently the guys I was partying with picked me up and threw me in the garbage. I remember my mother coming through the clinic doors where the ambulance took me. She was crying, and she held on to me real tight, screaming, 'My baby, my baby.' But I didn't feel like anyone's baby. I just felt like a piece of trash."

God the Father calls us his beloved sons and daughters. Satan calls us garbage.

Sophia tried to outrun the voices. She went to rehab more than twenty times. She tricked with the staff at some of the facilities. She was banned from others. The voices kept shouting, and she kept listening. And when she came out of rehab, she got high all over again. Every time.

Even her mother finally abandoned her. Sophia said, "She got tired of trying to save me, of coming to the dope houses and paying off the dealers and snatching me out. She was raising my daughters by herself, and at the same time I was stealing from her so I could keep getting high. I don't blame her for washing her hands of me. I finally got to the point where I wanted to die. I would try to overdose on any kind of pills I could get my hands on. But I would never die. I only got sick."

In 2006, Sophia married again. She was lonely and still so empty and thought maybe this man could give her the love she thought she was looking for. She stopped smoking crack because she was pregnant with her seventh child, a little boy she named Daniel—but the marriage was controlling and abusive.

After Daniel was born, Sophia began to drink every day. Ironically, she also began to frequent a church down the road that she passed every time she went to the liquor store or the dope house to get high. She told me she felt "drawn." She started attending, sometimes with her husband, and sometimes wearing sunglasses because of the black eyes he would give her when he beat her nearly to death.

And then one Sunday she fell on the altar in tears and just kept repeating, "I can't go on—I'm so, so tired." Sophia believes this was the moment she put her faith in Jesus. To use the common term, she was saved. It was a step—a huge step—but you can be saved and still be a wounded mess. By her own admission, though she now believed there was a God who would one day take her "to heaven," she still didn't know about a God who loved her right now. Her voices continued to shout that she was dirt.

It was a couple of more violent years until her marriage was finally over. In Sophia's own words, "The day Daniel's dad left me in October of 2008, I had seventy-nine dollars and seven or eight nickel rocks. I had little Daniel on my hip and was just coming from the dope house. My husband was in the parking lot of the apartment complex and saw me walking across the field. He shouted at me, 'Look at you. When is the last time you ate? Cleaned up? Did your nails?' He gave me his keys to the apartment and left. I went into the filthy hole we lived in and got high. Again."

And then, in a moment of unexplained grace, Sophia took an honest look at herself. Her rent was two months overdue. She and her baby were going to be put on the streets because she had smoked and drunk all the rent money. The drugs and alcohol had left her empty. She was totally alone. So she got down on her knees and cried out, "Lord, please, help me." Sophia finally surrendered—and after more than twenty years on the streets of Detroit, she began her journey home.

Sophia came to us at Hope Community Church soon after, sometime in 2009. She was a believer who had surrendered her life—but like many of us "surrendered believers," she was still overwhelmed by her pain. But then she began to hear about how much God loved her. How he was not just her King, but her Abba. How Jesus didn't come to give her rules to obey but to heal her broken heart and set her free from her chains and bondage. And how Jesus took her sorrow and pain upon his body at the Cross and wept with her now. She learned that he wanted more than anything to give her his beauty for her ashes and his oil of joy for her mourning (Isaiah 61:3).

The morning Sophia began to cry out to God in front of our church family, I think I was preaching from Psalm 13, one of the psalms of lament that God gave Israel to help her grieve and heal. Sophia couldn't hang on to her wounds any longer. Surrounded by the love and acceptance of the people of God, she began to pour out all of that pain at the feet of her loving Savior.

I've got to admit, I was a bit taken aback when Sophia stood up. I wasn't exactly sure what to do. So I simply stood there, silently and respectfully, asking God to "show me" while Sophia grieved decades of wounds.

And then the Holy Spirit took over. I have no other explanation. A sister named Cora stood up and grabbed the hand of my wife, Carla, for courage. Cora looked at all two hundred of us sitting in the sanctuary and said prophetically, "We've got to understand, Sophia is crying out from her bones." Then she proceeded to look directly at Sophia all the way across the room and told her that she had been sexually molested multiple times as a little girl. Cora had never spoken this truth publicly before.

She told Sophia that she wasn't trying to "fix" her. But she wanted Sophia to know that she truly understood. And that God had begun to meet her in her pain. Cora said, "Sophia, I don't know how long it is going to be before God heals me more completely—and I don't know how long it is going to be for you—but believe it, Sophia. He is with you. We are with you. And we will stay with you all the way through this process. We will stay with you all the way home. And some day, you're going to know joy. Some day it's going to be all right." I looked around the sanctuary at that moment and realized that most of us were weeping with these two sisters who wept with each other. This—this was real church.

Then the most amazing thing happened—Sophia's spirit and countenance changed. A moment before she had been shouting, literally screaming and sobbing out her pain with broken sentences and flailing arms. Now, through the empathy and compassion of a community of brothers and sisters, Sophia began to heal right before our eyes. She nodded at Cora, wiped her tears, slowly took her seat, and then looked at me as if to say, *It's okay now, Pastor. You can go on.* Sophia had shared a part of her wound that needed to be grieved that day, and as God's people wept with her, the healing of her broken heart began.

After that Sunday, Sophia grieved much more of her pain in small groups, counseling sessions, and personal times with the Father. In the same way, many of us will do much of our grieving with our Abba and with one another in more intimate settings—if we feel safe. But the point is that as Sophia grieved, slowly but surely her shaming voices began to recede into the background, and she began to hear the voice of her Abba calling her "my beloved daughter."

Grieving our pain happens in layers, like the melting of an iceberg. The growth and calming of the voices that come from grieving are more cyclical than linear, and there can be painful, fitful starts and stops along the way. About a year into her healing journey that began that Sunday morning, Sophia relapsed.

> I got high and then I got into a car with a guy who took me onto a dark street and told me to take off all my clothes. He told me he had a gun and he would kill me if I left. I said, "Please don't kill me. I have a son." And then I asked him, "Do you know Jesus?"

Even when the old, shaming voices come back, once our healing begins, the voice of the Father continues to speak his love. The man stopped and stared at those words, told her to put her clothes back on, robbed her of some money . . . and then let her go!

Sophia was filled with so much shame that she wailed and wailed—grieving this new attack from an enemy who never, ever sleeps. Sophia couldn't even come to church. She just couldn't. So that next Sunday we called her *from* church during the service. I held out the phone with the speaker on, and everyone shouted out, "We love you, Sophia!"

The following Sunday she was back. Head down, but back. And just a little bit more healed. Sophia told me, "I never want to feel this shame and separation from my Lover ever again. I've met Jesus, a *true* lover who I now know loves me *truly*. So I am never, ever going back out there." And she hasn't.

Sophia used to walk the street that runs right by the magnificent Masonic Temple in the middle of a tough neighborhood in Detroit. The Masonic Temple is the place where hundreds of people each year dress in their finest and go for birthdays and graduations and weddings and debutante balls. One day Sophia was stumbling, hung over, past the Masonic, watching folks in tuxedos and gowns walk up the steps.

"Pastor," she told me, "as I was walking, my head was down. I was filled with so much shame. The very night before I had turned tricks on the same steps these folks were using to get to their parties. I remember thinking, *You'll never have clothes like that, Sophia. You'll never be invited to experience that kind of joy. Because that's not who you are. You ain't nothin' but a crackhead ho. Those parties aren't for people like you.*

Then she said,

But you know what, Pastor? Do you know what God did? Just a few weeks ago, one of my friends from Hope invited me to go to a debutante ball—and guess where? The Masonic Temple! I told them I didn't have anything to wear, and they took me to buy a dress, a gown, the first one I have ever owned! And they bought my son a little suit so he could go with me.

And you know what God has been telling me? He's been saying, "Sophia, you're my little girl. I love you. I have always loved you. And you do belong at the party—you've always belonged at the party. You just didn't know it before. That's why you walked the streets. You didn't know how precious you are. You didn't know what you know now, that you are mine."

Pastor, don't you see? He has always loved me! I have always been his! And now, finally, I know it— and I can finally hear his voice telling me that it's true.

And the next Sunday morning, when Sophia shared her story in front of the church, do you know what she wore? You guessed it. She wore her new gown.

So what about you? Have you struggled to hear the Father's voice whispering, "I love you—I love you so very, very much"? Maybe the voices of pain and shame shout so loudly that you can't see or hear your Abba calling you his beloved daughter, beloved son. Maybe it's time to let the tears flow and to let your Father, who is so lovingly near, hold you while you cry. Then joy will come . . . in the morning.

Chapter 6

SHAME

_____

When you experience shame . . . [i]t is as if you are standing
alone on one side of a broken bridge while everyone
else in the world stares at you from the other side.
SANDRA D. WILSON, *Released from Shame*

They looked to Him and were radiant,
And their faces were not ashamed.
PSALM 34:5, NKJV

SOPHIA'S STORY REMINDS US that we must grieve in order to
heal. But it also reminds us of the insidious, deadly power
of an emotion called shame. The voices from Sophia's past
shouted that she didn't just do bad stuff—she was bad stuff.
That she didn't just make mistakes—she was a mistake.

These voices are the collective voice of shame. Shame tells
us that we are unworthy of love and acceptance. Shame is
what each of us experience if we are not experiencing the
love of the Father.

This shame is pathological—and dark. It's "an irrational sense of defectiveness, a feeling not of having crossed
to the wrong side of the boundary but of having been born

there . . . . It is the self regarding the self with the withering and unforgiving eye of contempt."[4]

So this isn't mere embarrassment, the almost laughable shame we all feel when we trip up the stairs. It's also not the healthy, moral shame that Adam and Eve felt in the Garden when their wrongdoing was exposed. Most importantly, pathological shame is different from guilt. Guilt is about *what I do*. Shame is about *who I am*. The antidote for guilt is forgiveness. Shame calls me to cease to exist.

How many of us have invoked the promise of 1 John 1:9 after a screwup of one kind or another, confessing our sin and believing that God has forgiven us through Christ? And yet, even with the truth of that timeless passage of Scripture staring us in the face, we feel like dirt. Knowing that we are forgiven but still feeling dirty is pathological shame.

From the moment of our conception, God is calling us by name and telling us how much he loves us. But every time Satan looks at us and opens his lying mouth, pathological shame spews out. He wants to saturate the God-shaped vacuum inside every human heart with the life-sucking message that we're not worth anything.

Worthless is exactly how June Walker felt for most of her life. June's destructive journey with shame began in childhood. That's where it begins for most of us, really— for better or worse, our parents give us a deep impression of who we are before we're able to discern our identity for ourselves. June's dad left when she was two, and as a child she always wondered why. Was she not enough? Of course, that wasn't the reason. After June's dad laid his hands on her mom one too many times, her mom got a gun, put it to his head, and threatened to pull the trigger. So he left for Arkansas and never came back. June didn't find all this out until years later, long after shame had permeated her vulnerable spirit.

Then there was the shame of poverty. After June's dad left, she and her mom moved in with her grandmother, and they were very, very poor. June deeply appreciated the way her mother sacrificed to try to feed and clothe her, but having next to nothing often made her feel like nothing.

Way more significant in terms of shame, however, were "the beatings." First, Mom and Grandma would take June to church, where "she got emotionally beaten with the Bible." June says this is where she first began to hate religion. The very place intended by God to be the dispensary of his deep and everlasting love is often the arena where many of us are inundated with more shame. And then, June remembers, they would come home from church, and she'd be beaten with an extension cord or hanger—or worse, "the cat of nine tails," a bullwhip made of leather.

"Grandma would grab you, stand on your neck, and then whip you," June told me. "Or she would put your head between her ankles and whip you as my grandfather sat there watching and laughing the entire time. My mom and grandma would tell me they loved me even before they beat me over and over, but I remember saying to myself, 'If you love me, how can you keep beating the crap out of me?'"

Most of the time, June didn't feel love in her home. But she did feel saturated with shame.

On top of the poverty and beatings, throughout June's childhood she was bullied. She had a congenital heart condition and was so skinny that kids would make fun of her and try to beat her up. More shame. If it isn't the home or church, it's the school, the community, or the culture telling us we aren't smart enough, tall enough, strong enough, good enough, or beautiful enough. Try as we may to compensate or change, we still feel worthless.

Finally, the beatings and bullying, the fact that there was never enough food, no dad, no money, and no love, took their toll on June. At the age of sixteen, overwhelmed by shame, June began smoking weed, using angel dust (the killer hallucinogen PCP), and drinking massive quantities of cheap wine.

Shame doesn't force us to do anything, but the psychic pain of feeling worthless can be so intense that we'll do anything to make it stop. And the moment the high of drugs, alcohol, work, achievement, sex, applause, religion, money, power, or whatever finally wears off, the shame comes roaring back more potent than before. Not only do we feel the original shame but also the shame of the addictive, failed attempt to make the shame go away. And so we try again. By the time June went to college at Michigan State University in 1975, she was living this shame cycle around the clock.

At MSU, June's shame began to escalate. As an African American raised almost exclusively in the black community in Detroit, June saw more white people on her first day at Michigan State than she had ever seen at one time in her entire life. Racial fear and hatred didn't take long to shout at June that she was "less than" simply because of her skin color. As she was moving into the dorm, she noticed her white roommate making a phone call. Later in the day her roommate's parents showed up and moved her out.

"They never said a word, never made eye contact," June said. The next day June saw her former roommate in the cafeteria. She told June, "Hey, it isn't because you're black." But June knew the truth.

It only takes one well-timed racial incident to traumatize someone's spirit. But there was so much more to come. In the days ahead, June and her new black roommate were often called the N-word. More than once they had water dumped on them as they walked out of the dorm on the way to class. One day their suitemates—white boys, June told me—asked June and her roommate, "When are you girls going to clean up the bathroom like our maids used to clean ours when we were kids?" Sometimes it even got physical. June would simply be walking down the hall and get purposely bumped into the wall by a white student for no apparent reason. Except, of course, that she was black.

June's African American roommate eventually left school. She couldn't take the abuse. But June stayed. One day she and an African American girlfriend were in an elevator with a white guy who asked them if they "grew tails at night so they could swing from trees." Shame-based people, no matter the color of their skin, will say anything about anyone to feel better about themselves. Ignorant, demeaning, racist language and behavior always comes from the heart of someone who struggles with pathological shame. We can only give what we have received. If I'm hating on you, it's because inside my heart, I'm already hating on me.

June and her friend beat the white guy in the elevator. A few weeks later, June beat up her RA. When the student court asked her why she hadn't told anyone about all the racial abuse, she said she didn't know. But I know. Shame shuts you down and takes away your voice. We think, *Who wants to hear me, a worthless person, telling my worthless story?* Vulnerably confessing pain may be perceived as weakness. We think it's best to not say a word and keep on numbing and doing whatever we must do to keep the pain at bay.

In her junior year, one holiday break after everyone had gone home, June found herself in her room, all alone, crying uncontrollably.

"I hated white people," she told me. "I wasn't trying to hate them, because even with all the mess in my home, we weren't taught to hate. But I did hate them, and I didn't know how to stop. But most of all, I hated myself. That night I cried all night long."

June's anger and drug use descended to a whole new level. She started using other hallucinogens, slurping codeine, and ingesting a slew of uppers and downers. Somehow June still managed to graduate in 1979 with a degree in criminal justice. Then, in 1980, she enrolled in law school at the

University of Detroit. She wanted to be the first black female Supreme Court justice, and I believe she had the gifts to do just that. But shame eventually sucks the life out of our potential. The love of the Father fills and gives us everything we need to be our true selves and to give our lives away to others. But the shame of the enemy empties us so that we've got nothing for anyone else.

In 1983, June's second year of law school, her mother died after a horrifying and painful battle with stomach cancer. In spite of the beatings and shame, June still loved her mom, and her death tore June apart. Soon she was homeless.

Over the next twenty-four years, June was homeless seven more times. She had three abortions and two miscarriages. She gave birth to Cierra and Courtney, two daughters she lost custody of on three separate occasions. All she wanted to do was get high. She became a prostitute to fund her habit. Johns raped her more times than she could count. She didn't care whether she lived or died. Because that's what shame does. It steals our will to live and convinces us that relief will only come when we cease to exist. Don't forget: Our enemy isn't playing. He's trying to kill us, and shame is his poison—a slow, lethal drip that gets into our emotional and spiritual cells and vacuums our God-given humanity and love of life right out of us.

There were so, so many times when June almost died. Like the time when she smoked the rock she was supposed to sell and the john put a gun to her head but for some reason didn't pull the trigger. Or the time she was at the house of one of her "tricking" friends and heard a voice—June swears it was God—telling her, "You need to go home. Right now." She picked her two-year-old daughter Courtney up off the floor, walked out the door, and got on a bus. The next day, when June went back to the friend's house, she found her in a closet, crack pipe still in her hand. She had been doused with gasoline and set on fire.

That wasn't the only time June almost lost one of the girls. In 1991, she went to jail in Southfield for trying to rob a store. She didn't tell anyone she left Courtney alone in the house with a bottle in her mouth. For two days. Luckily—June calls it "grace"—a guy who had been staying with her found Courtney and took her to her auntie's house.

"Pastor," June told me, "some people don't want to believe it, but folks 'out there' hear from God. He knows they're running from him, choking on shame, and so he pursues them and chases them and shouts mercy to them, trying to save them because he loves them so much."

He's shouting mercy to some of us right now. We're "out there" in our own far country of shame, but he's right behind us, pursuing us, refusing to let us go. And he's calling us to start releasing the shame and to begin our journey home to the healing power of his love.

A couple of times in these decades on the street, June tried to save herself. Like the time in 1988 when she thought if she could just get out of Detroit she would be all right. She won a scholarship to the University of the District of Columbia School of Law—but in a week, she had smoked it all away. She stayed at a student friend's apartment while the friend was gone, and when she ran out of money, she sold everything in the girl's apartment to get more dope. The law school didn't kick June out. They offered her rehab. But she went back to the streets of Detroit, where she spent nineteen more years running from shame.

We can't wish shame away. We can't pray it away. And we can't make it go away with just a little more effort or a few successes or even a supposed "new start." Pathological shame roots deep into our spirits and makes its home there. And it will stay there, influencing all our emotions and choices and relationships—until it is healed. Shame needs healing. Shame needs a Healer. And in 2006, when June finally hit bottom, her Healer, her true Love, was there to take her hand.

She was tricking and working the door in a crack house on Detroit's west side. Courtney and Cierra had just been taken from her for the third time, and protective services told her, "You will never see your kids again." June had lost hope. Shame's death wish was knocking at her door.

June asked the guy who owned the house if she could use his pistol. She went to the store to get some booze. Her plan was to come back to the crack house, get wasted, and put the gun to her head. But on the corner of Lahser and Grand River, the Healer showed up—in the form of a few women "laughing and carrying on" at the bus stop.

"What are you about?" June asked them.

"We stay at Genesis House III," one of the women told her. "They're helping us get our lives together and stay off the streets." They told her how to get in touch, and she borrowed one of their cell phones and called. The voice at the other end said, "Girl, call us back today, and we'll send a van to come and get you!" June went home, and she didn't call back.

But she also didn't pull the trigger.

June continued to trick and use, but every few weeks she would call Genesis House to make sure they were still there. Finally, about six months later, June found her way back to the bus stop, hoping to see the sisters sitting there again. She couldn't remember the last time she had combed her hair, and she hadn't showered for what seemed like a year. She was wearing a shirt, jeans, raggedy shoes with no shoelaces, and no underwear.

The women weren't there. But it didn't matter because her Abba showed up—again—this time in the person of a bus driver who pulled up and opened the door as if to let her in. But before she stepped on the bus, June asked him, "Sir, can you take me to the intake center at Herman Kiefer? I need to get into treatment."

"Are you an addict?" the bus driver asked.

And for the first time ever, June said, "Yes, I am."

Shame keeps us from admitting our truth. But the very minute we courageously say, "This is my reality—but I don't want to live like this anymore," we've chosen to take our first step toward home.

The driver took June to Joy Road on Detroit's west side, personally escorted her to yet another bus, and told the new driver to take her to Herman Kiefer. When she finally got off the second bus, everyone on board clapped. June thought it was because she smelled so bad, but the second bus driver said, "No. They just want you to get the help you need."

When June walked into Herman Kiefer, the guy at the desk said that all the pipes had just burst and they weren't taking anyone till at least the next day. Defeated, June turned around to walk out. And then the intake guy said, "Hey, you, come here. I'm going to take you anyway." At that very moment, for the first time in her life, June thought, *God is here*. I matter to him. And he's got me. A van transported her to the Detroit Rescue Mission to begin her ninety days of detox, and it was there that June Walker, beloved daughter of God, fell into her Father's arms.

Three months later, June arrived at Genesis House III. "Such a peace came over me there," she said. "I told myself I was going to do everything these folks told me to do. I was going to learn how to stay clean and hopefully get my kids back." Soon after this particular moment of surrender, June heard a clear-as-a-bell voice say, "You will get your kids back, June. That's a promise." And a few years later, Courtney and Cierra came home.

In her third or fourth month at Genesis House III, June began to believe that her destiny was not to die as a shame-based, beat-up junkie but somehow to live giving glory to Jesus. She began to believe that she never needed to use again. It was also at Genesis House III that June first heard and understood that Jesus died—for her. She had heard the words of the story before at her grandma's church, but they meant nothing to her. Shame keeps us from personalizing and taking into our hearts anything about God that gives us value and allows us to know, to feel, and to be secured in his love.

Larry and Marilyn Johnson, two volunteers who had only recently been discovering the personal love of the Father for themselves, were the first to tell June that Jesus loved her so much that he came to die specifically for her. And then the Johnsons brought June to Hope Community Church on a morning when I "just happened" to be preaching about the intimate love of God for each of us. June told me that at first it was hard to listen to me—let alone look at me—because I was white. But over the course of the next two hours as we all sat, sang, prayed, and listened to the Word together, it began to matter less and less what color I was. She felt something genuine and authentic coming from my heart and the hearts of those sitting around her.

You can't fake the love of the Father. You can speak eloquent words about God's love, but if the truth that those words represent is only lodged in your intellect, then the words are hollow. But when you begin to really know his love deep in your spirit, you can stammer, stumble, and ramble, and it won't make a difference. The power isn't in the presentation—but in the reality of the love of God itself.

June remembers me saying over and over to the entire community that morning, "God loves you. He really, really loves you." But to June, it was as if I were saying it only to her. And the shame of forty-five years of self-hatred and self-harm began to be deeply healed on an emotional level by her Father's love.

I remember that day. I remember meeting June for the very first time. But I don't remember preaching especially well or the music being especially powerful or anything particularly special happening. But that's the point. Shame isn't healed by the spectacular. Please don't forget Peter's truth: "Love each other deeply, because love covers over a multitude of sins" (1 Peter 4:8). The love of the Father, cycled through the living body of Jesus Christ, freely given in vulnerable relationship, has the power to heal anything and everything perpetrated by our enemy. Even decades of death-dealing shame.

For the last eight years, June has been in the process of healing, of living the long, sometimes slow process of letting God love her. This is how the healing of shame usually goes. Pathological shame isn't a ten-day spiritual virus, easily healed by a little time, rest, fluids, and a few Bible verses. It's an insidious emotional and spiritual cancer. Shame is at the heart of the cosmic spiritual battle between God and Satan for the precious life of every human being.

Remember, in some of his last words on the planet, Jesus said, "Love one another as I have loved you. Then the world will know that you are with me . . . and they will know that I come from God" (John 13:34-35; 17:21-23, author's paraphrase). If we aren't in the process of healing from shame, then our shame is shutting us off from really knowing the love of the Father. And if we don't know his love, we can't love anyone else, even our brothers and sisters in Christ. Saturated in shame, followers of Jesus will continue to divide and hate over race, gender, ethnicity, minor doctrinal differences and denominational nuances, music, carpet color, politics, and other assorted nonsense. The division will be blamed on altruistic motives like "keeping the faith pure from heresy." But the real reason behind the splits and factions? Unhealed shame. And the world will only see a fractured, broken, bleeding-out Jesus. They will never see the whole, powerful, life-giving Jesus who wants to heal their sin, pain, and shame.

Healing from shame isn't just about how it makes us feel. It's literally about the Kingdom of God coming to earth. It's about God setting us free to love other devastated, shame-based sons and daughters all the way home to his Father heart. Today, even as she continues to heal from a life of shame, June Walker, daughter of God, leads our prison ministry. Increasingly filled with the love of the Father, June spearheads a team of twenty-five volunteers, who over the last four years have served fifty prisoners in fifteen different state and federal prisons.

Satan must be sick to his stomach. He had June by the throat—locked down in shame, poisoning herself with drugs, and giving her body away to haters. But now this former captive is helping set other captives free.

How many of us still believe the lie that our destiny is the living death of shame? We may not shoot heroin or turn tricks to dull the pain. Maybe we just live perpetually sad because we hate ourselves and don't know who to tell or how to get free. Or maybe we live in a painful prison where we lift our hands to sing praise about the personal love of God and don't believe a word of it. Perhaps we've buried ourselves in our career, hoping for small life-giving hits of approval. Or maybe we're slaved through three degree programs, praying that someday we might feel like we're okay because of special letters by our name. For some, hopping from bed to bed provides short-term relief but never long-term peace. Others of us live our lives avoiding our reflection in a mirror or any kind of intimate, vulnerable conversation that might reveal our deep insecurity. Still others hide behind an obnoxious veneer of pride when inside our hearts we simply long to know that we are deeply loved.

In other words, I'm wondering how many of us reading June's story are saturated with shame, struggling to even talk to God for a second because we can hardly believe he really wants to connect with, love, and embrace the likes of us. The Father is calling to you through June's story, shouting with tears through the darkness, "I love you, daughter. I love you, son. I miss you so much. I want us to walk together. My arms around you, my love saturating your heart. It's time for you to choose . . . to come home."

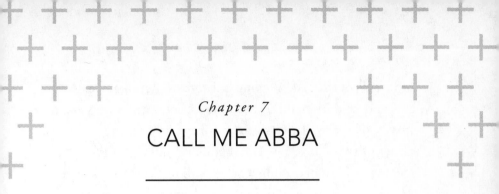

Chapter 7

CALL ME ABBA

All children want to love their fathers—and to
have fathers who love them in return.
DR. PAUL C. VITZ, *Faith of the Fatherless*

You did not receive the spirit of slavery leading again to fear, but you
received the Spirit of adoption, by whom we cry, "Abba, Father."
ROMANS 8:15, NET

MY FRIEND DAVE WAS DYING. Cancer. As I sat beside him in
the weeks before he breathed his last, my sense is that he was
ready to go—but he wrestled with death because of his love
for his best friend and wife, Cathy, and also because of his
kids. Dave loved his kids so deeply. He fought to stay with
them. He fought to keep them from the pain of being forced
to let him go. He fought because he loved them so very, very
much.

During one morning visit, I watched Bria—a successful
married businesswoman from New York City—snuggle up
close to her daddy in his hospital bed, much like she would
have as a little girl. Her younger sister, Erika, was lying on the

other side of the bed, weeping quietly as she stroked her dad's arm and held his hand. A few days earlier, I quietly observed Dave's firstborn, Troy—former college athlete and married father of two—take his dad's hand and hold it in the interlocking fashion of a young couple walking in the park. Then Troy leaned into his dad's ear and whispered something. I'm not sure what. But the intimacy, the devotion, the heart connection between these two strong men were unmistakable and unforgettable.

Just days before Dave slipped into the arms of his God, Erika said to my wife, Carla, "My dad raised me to believe in myself and to be independent. But I will always, always need my dad."

Indeed.

Watching my courageous friend with his children reminds me of a profound but often neglected truth: Everyone, absolutely everyone, needs a loving father. When someone doesn't have a dad—or has a dad who doesn't love them well—the results are often disastrous. Prisons are full of men and women who will tell you that their brokenness began with "no dad" or a "broken dad." And it's not an accident that if you google "the impact of absent fathers," hundreds of thousands of articles will appear. Both Joseph Stalin and Adolph Hitler were beaten by their fathers. Mao Zedong's dad was known as a tyrant. My friend Brian's dad didn't really "see" him, Kennell's and Melissa's fathers ignored them, and Samson, Sophia, and June never even knew their dads.

I have also come to believe a second truth: All who don't

have a dad who loves them well are either consciously or unconsciously looking for a loving father. A couple of years ago, after speaking at a Wayne State University Cru meeting, I talked and prayed with an incredibly gifted young college student named Mike. He shared some of his painful story, and we decided to start hanging out. Over the next couple of months, after only a few hours of connection, he spontaneously started calling me "pops" for no apparent reason. He doesn't know me all that well. But he's emotionally disconnected from his earthly dad, and like everyone else, he's looking for a father to love him.

Last summer I met a young woman named Teah at a camp in Wisconsin where I was doing some staff training. She, too, poured out her heart. By the end of the week, Teah was calling me "papa"—and again, I really don't get why, except that she's emotionally disconnected from her dad and looking for a loving father. Pradeep, a twentysomething pre-med student wrote me a few months after an initial cup of coffee and said, "Pastor Kevin, the first time we hung out, you told me you wish you had been my father and I had been your son. You told me that you loved me. No one had ever spoken to me like that before. For the next month, I thought about those words every night—and cried." Sue—former heroin addict, three times married, and mother of two sons and a daughter—calls me "her spiritual dad."

Teah is Caucasian, Mike is African American, and Pradeep is from India. And Sue is just one year younger than me. Ethnicity is a nonissue. Age is a nonissue. Love from a father's heart transcends color, culture, and gray hair. It also doesn't matter to Mike, Teah, Pradeep, or Sue that I'm not perfect or that I sometimes failed and continue to fail as a dad with my own three daughters. What matters is that I sincerely listen to their hearts, embrace their story, and give them just a bit of what God the Father has given me—his deep and unconditional love. Because not only does everyone need a loving father—each of us is looking for one as well.

But what blows me away is a third truth: The main way God chooses to reveal himself to us in the New Testament . . . is as a loving Father.

The Old Testament is subtle in its references to God as a personal Father. Of course, he is described as Israel's Father (Exodus 4:22; Deuteronomy 32:6; Isaiah 63:16) at several key moments in her history—but Abraham, Moses, and David never called him *their* Father. And while there are certainly many rich and textured Old Testament images of God loving Israel as Father—like Isaiah's moving picture of God inscribing our names on the palm of his hand to show that he never, ever forgets us—explicit textual references are admittedly few. But this reality only serves to magnify how the concept of God as a personal Father explodes onto the pages of the New Testament—especially through the words and life of Jesus of Nazareth.

When Jesus comes out of obscurity to be baptized by his cousin John and begin his ministry, the first voice he hears is God the Father saying, "This is my beloved Son, with whom I am well pleased" (Matthew 3:17, ESV). And amazingly, for the rest of his three years on the planet, almost every time Jesus talks about God, he calls him Father. In the Sermon on the Mount, Jesus uses the term "God" six times, "Lord" three times, and "King" once. But he refers to God as "Father" seventeen times. In John's Gospel alone, Jesus calls God "Father" more than one hundred and ten times and "my Father" twenty-five times. And of course, in the most desperate, frightened moment of his life, in the Garden of Gethsemane on the night before he was crucified, Jesus cries out to God as "Abba"—an Aramaic term that implies deep intimacy, maybe even the intimacy a young Hebrew child feels for his or her dad.

Here is where all of this truth about God as Father gets deeply personal. Paul says it like this:

> You did not receive the spirit of slavery leading again to fear, but you received the Spirit of adoption, by whom *we* cry, "Abba, Father."
> ROMANS 8:15, NET, EMPHASIS ADDED

In other words, this isn't just about Jesus. It's about us, too. Obviously, God is our Creator, Lord, and King—but we are invited to call him Abba, just like Jesus, and to relate to him primarily as our intimate Father. In fact, Paul implies that if we want to know God's love, we must know him as Abba—the Father who cares about us so much that he walked into the cosmic spiritual orphanage one day, picked us out of a crowd, and chose us to be his sons and daughters.

Despite our baggage and our mess, our issues and our sin, he wants us. He longs for us because he loves us.

Finally, all these father truths converge and connect: The loving Father we're all really looking for is God. Only his perfect Father love can fill the vacuum in our hearts. But the wounding image of even well-meaning earthly fathers is often so pervasive and overpowering that it distorts and disables, keeping us from experiencing the love of our Abba. When we look to his face for healing (Psalm 34:5), what if all we can see is the wounding face of our earthly dad? The wounding voice of our earthly father can shout so loudly to our spirit and heart that we literally aren't able to hear the voice of our Abba. In fact, my own disconnect from the experience of my Abba's love began with my early sense that I was disconnected from my earthly father's heart.

I want to make one thing extremely clear: My dad is not a bad man. He's a truth-teller—he doesn't lie. He has been faithful to my mother over the years, even through some major drama in their marriage. He's practiced law in his home community for close to five decades, working really hard to feed me, put clothes on my back, pay for my college education, and much more. Over the years my dad has actively and sacrificially helped hundreds of human beings of all ages, backgrounds, ethnicities, and cultures. He is generous with his money, never misses Sunday worship, taught adult Sunday School for years, preached in dozens of churches, chaired elder boards, sat on ministry teams, and counseled young couples in trouble. He was a top legislator in the Indiana State Senate for eight years, championing causes that matter to families, often facing persecution for simply standing tall for what he believed in. He even started a baseball league when I was sixteen primarily so I would have a place to play once I was too old for my other team! Today, at eighty-two, my father continues to bless his entire family financially, works at loving my mother even more deeply, is a solid grandfather, and prays for all of us every day without exception. He was and is a good man. And all of these pieces of virtue in my father have helped shape the man I am today. I will be forever grateful for the various aspects of character that my father downloaded into me by his example—not just through his words, but by the way he has lived his life.

But here's what my dad didn't do—what I desperately needed him to do, but I don't think he knew how to do: My dad didn't connect with my heart. That may not sound like a big deal. But most of what is core about us, what moves, impacts, and motivates us, happens in our hearts. Our deep feelings about ideas, circumstances, the past or the future, relationships, God, and ourselves are the most powerful force in our lives. We are created in God's image, and heartfelt emotion is central to who we are. It isn't too strong to say that if you miss a person's heart, you likely miss the person. And this is never more true than with the heart of a child.

A psychologist once interviewed dozens and dozens of folks in his practice, asking, "What do you wish your dad would have done more when you were a kid?" One of the top five responses was, "I wish my dad had let me see his tears."

Another was, "I wish my dad had connected more deeply with my pain." If a father is going to truly know his son or daughter, he must tune in to their emotional core. He must connect with their heart.

Heart connection has always been a struggle for my dad. He was never much into feelings. Emotional pain especially seemed to make him uncomfortable. Unfortunately, I carried pervasive emotional pain deep inside my heart, a good portion of which was inadvertently poured into me by my mother. She'd had an extremely difficult childhood, filled with neglect, abuse, shame, and absolutely no sense of belonging or "home." At eighteen she met my father; thirteen days later they were engaged, and in a few months they were married. I was born nine and a half months after the wedding, and the unconscious downloading of my mother's lifetime of confusion and shame began.

I have tears coming out of my eyes as I write—not just because of my childhood pain but because my mom has changed so much over the years and has much regret about the screaming and the hitting and the threatening and the shame she poured into my spirit. When I was a teenager, I remember hearing her more than once crying out to God and begging for forgiveness and help after a rage-filled episode with her kids. I truly believe my mom wanted to love well. In fact, when she read this chapter, she reminded me that as a kid I asked lots of questions and that often she would point me to an answer from the Scripture—because she loved me so much. And I know it's true. It's also true that later in life my mother began to engage the love of the Father at a deeper level and became a wounded healer of many in her community.

But, as a sensitive firstborn kid, I became the repository of her pathological shame. My wounds revealed themselves in workaholic perfectionism and guilt, a deep loneliness and feeling that no one truly liked me, a sense that there was something intrinsically wrong with me, and a self-hatred that manifested in a sadness that I lived with every day of my life. I developed intense anger and deep-seated rage that was mostly directed at . . . myself.

My dad never understood. He used to say, "Look at how God has blessed you, son! Let me tell you what it was like to really hurt—back in the day when your mom and I were first married and had next to nothing." He never really understood the aloneness either. For example, during one particularly difficult time in my sophomore year of high school, he advised, "If you don't feel like a part of the basketball team, then man up and talk to the coach." These unintentionally insensitive words made me feel more alone than ever.

But my father absolutely never even began to understand the deep feeling of rage that was inside me all day, all night, every moment of every week of every year. "Why are you so angry, son?" he asked me often. But I think his question was unconsciously rhetorical—he usually quickly followed with, "Stop being angry. I'm not angry. You shouldn't be angry either." When we tell people not to feel, we are basically telling them they are stupid for feeling that way in the first place.

And, of course, that's exactly how his dismissive attitude made me feel—stupid, ridiculous, like an emotional loser.

One time when I was nine, I struck out in a Little League game and got so mad—mostly at myself, of course—that I yelled, threw the bat, and started to cry. As I walked back to the dugout, I remember longing for someone to come and put a blanket over me and hide me from the shaming glances of the crowd or to at least put their arm around me and tell me it was going to be all right. But instead, my dad simply shouted, "Either you get a grip on yourself, or I promise you I'm going to jerk you off the team."

Then there were the times when my mom would shout her shame into my young world and I would instinctively yell back at her. Instead of trying to understand my heart, my dad would only threaten me with some kind of megapunishment, saying over and over again something ridiculous like, "She may not always be right, but she's always your mother." The last time this happened, I was sixteen. My dad ordered me to bend over the couch in front of my mom and younger siblings, and he hit me with his hand on my backside over and over, as if I were a wicked six-year-old. I wanted my dad to listen. I wanted him to hear my heart about how many years my wounded mother had puked her pain into my life. I didn't need him to sign off on any disrespectful behavior on my part—I simply, desperately needed him to connect with my sixteen-year-old emotional core.

Of course, I now know that my dad did what he did because he was clueless and felt out of control. He was given few tools for parenting by his own Christian, church attending, decent, hard-working but also clueless father—so I get it. I really do. But it's difficult to describe the devastating impact of that kind of humiliating, shaming moment on a young man's heart. Even as I write these words, my physical heart is beating in my chest so hard and fast that it feels like I'm reliving the embarrassing trauma of forty-four years ago. Listen carefully—I'm not telling this story to embarrass my father or to unnecessarily relive my own pain. I simply want to illustrate how even a good and decent man, a good and moral father, can completely miss his son's or daughter's heart. Perhaps it isn't accidental that the apostle Paul warned dads about fathering in such a way that his kids become "discouraged"—a Greek word that could also be translated as "lose heart" (Colossians 3:21).

Don't miss this. Many of us don't have dads who physically abandoned us, beat us with coat hangers, touched us inappropriately, or burned us with cigarettes after a weekend alcoholic binge. For many of us, the damage is so much more subtle: dads who always got up to go to work, played in softball leagues, sat in church services, worked in the garden, went on fishing trips, served at the Rescue Mission—and yet lived largely, if not completely, disconnected from their own hearts and from ours. And the results can be devastating, especially when it comes to our relationship with a God who calls himself our Father.

Look, I'm not saying my father didn't love me. He did and does. And I'm not saying your dad didn't love you or want to connect with your heart. But the truth is—and maybe this is your truth as well—my father never did connect with my heart. What he did connect with was my shame-based, over-achieving perfectionism.

When I was growing up, my dad worked all . . . the . . . time. He worked many Saturdays and always had a briefcase full of files he pulled out to work on when there was no other work to be done. I'm really thankful my dad wasn't a deadbeat and that he provided for us. But most of the time, all I wanted was for him to sit down and be with me. I think it would have made me feel like he liked me—not for "doing," but just for "being" myself. But often, even when he did come home, it was, "Hey son, there are chores to do. Let's get to it."

I have only two memories of my dad ever hanging out with me clearly just to "be" with me. The first was when he took a walk with me in the country when I was about nine, complete with a picnic lunch. It was amazing. I have a vivid memory of the dirt road, the hot sun, the quiet sense of simply being together. I remember finding an old toy rifle in a ditch, rusty with all the paint scratched off, and I remember fantasizing that I had discovered some abandoned WWII treasure. For the next year or so, when I played army with my buddies, it was my favorite gun—I think in part because I found it with my dad.

The other time was maybe a year later when my father worked hard to get me ready to go on a Scout-type fishing trip. I remember him hunting feverishly around the house for a functional fishing reel, taking the time to get it fixed on my rod, and making sure I had what I needed to enjoy the weekend. I remember watching him wrestle with how the rod was supposed to attach to the reel and thinking, *My dad really cares about my fishing trip. My dad really cares about me.* To this day, when I think about those two memories, tears come to my eyes.

One thing my father always did was show up whenever I was performing, whether academically, spiritually, or in sports. His dad never came to any of his ball games, so my dad decided he would always show up for his kids when they performed—and believe me, I appreciate it to this very moment. My father followed me around the Midwest for four years during my college football career, rarely missing a game. He even walked five miles on an Easter Sunday morning when I was fourteen years old to hear me preach my first sermon (he'd accidentally locked his keys in his car). However, in deep ways, my father's well-meaning attendance at every "performance" essentially backfired. It seemed as though my father loved me mostly when I was "doing." So I became a performer and an overachiever, unconsciously hoping that one day my dad would love me and want to be with me, even if I achieved absolutely nothing.

Then, over the years, my dad's face became God's face. My dad didn't connect with the pain in my heart—so in my mind, neither did God. My dad apparently loved me most when I performed, so clearly, God did as well. My heavenly Father couldn't possibly love me or want to be close to me when I was sad or lonely or especially when I was angry. But man, when I was doing something for the Kingdom—when I was a shining light for Jesus—God was front and center, smiling and applauding. Sure, God loved me. He loved me like my dad loved me. So, my response as a child and all the way into adulthood was to hide my pain from God and perform for God—until I began to break.

The first "breaking" occurred when I was twenty-three. My anger had thankfully been somewhat channeled into football for a decade. When football ended, I got married to my best friend, Carla. Six months in we had an argument. Carla got in my face like my mother used to, and I went nuts. I grabbed the petite and tender body and spirit of the love of my life and pushed her down with such force that she slid across the living room of our ten-by-forty mobile home. Carla almost left me that night. I wouldn't have blamed her if she did.

But God intervened. He whispered to me, not in an actual audible voice, but to my spirit in a way that was clear and unmistakable: "This isn't about Carla, son. This is about you and your empty heart. It's time for you to begin to heal. Step one—own your stuff. Own the vacuum in your spirit. Own the anger and insecurity, and tell Carla you are taking responsibility for finding out what the mess inside you is all about. Ask her to stay. And let's you and me start the journey to wholeness."

That night, kneeling alongside Carla on that green and orange shag carpet, our heads buried together in a matching green and orange sofa, my sometimes-halting, long journey home to my Abba began. I owned the mess and began to blindly take my first healing steps. The next morning I went to church and got prayer from the elders, and the morning after that I was in a counselor's office trying to figure out the source of my rage. I never abusively touched Carla again. But it took another thirteen years of Exodus-type wandering before the second major "break" occurred—my almost intentional face-to-face with a highway cement embankment. And I finally got it: I had missed God. I had believed in God but never really known him. It was time for this son to finally choose to come home from the far country to his Abba's heart.

This is where father-wound healing begins for most of us—when we're broken or breaking. In our brokenness, we start to heal by stopping the finger-pointing and by refusing to blame anyone, anywhere, anymore for our own emptiness. We start to heal by acknowledging how absolutely desperate we are to know and really feel the love of God. We start to heal by seeing the connection between the way our fathers either did or didn't attend to our hearts and how we have come to view and experience God as our Father. And finally, we start to heal by believing that if we don't heal from our earthly father wounds, it will be almost impossible to hear God the Father's voice calling us his beloved.

I don't know if you have a father-disconnect in your spirit or not. Not everyone does. But if you do, embracing this reality can be a difficult step. Many of us seem afraid to go there. Maybe we feel it would be disrespectful or unspiritual. Maybe we think our dads are too fragile for us to call out how they may have wounded us. Or maybe we wonder if this kind of work will really change anything in the long run. Look, I can't predict your future. But this I know: Jesus said he came to heal the brokenhearted and set the captive free. If you don't call out what the enemy has used from your well-meaning earthly dad to keep you from knowing the deep love of your heavenly Father, your life will never change and your heart will never be filled.

After my near suicide attempt, I knew I had to connect with God as my Abba but had no clue how or where to begin. So I simply asked God to show me—to reveal to me where the enemy had used life, culture, and even my earthly father to lie to me about who he really is. I asked him to begin to show me how he really loves me and how to really connect with him for the first time.

This is also your next step. Ask. You may have asked your earthly father for all kinds of connection and love, and for whatever reason he may have never responded. But I'm begging you—take a risk to believe that your heavenly Father isn't like that. Ask him to begin to heal your damaged spiritual eyes, to heal your distorted vision of his face toward you, and to help you see him as he really is: a Father who loves you passionately and unconditionally and longs to have you home. Take a risk. Ask.

One of the ways God began to heal me was a surprise. The Gospels began to come alive to me in ways that touched broken places in my spirit. I read Jesus' tale of the prodigal's father in Luke 15 as if for the very first time—finally realizing the Father's been standing at the window watching and waiting for me! He's running down the lane to embrace me! He's not angry—he's full of compassion for me. He's not asking me to perform or make up for lost time or jump through any spiritual hoops or even pay him back—but instead he's kissing me and giving me his signet ring and sandals and a special robe! My Father loves me, and he really, really wants me home.

Then I read about Jesus loving the nameless murderer crucified next to him—and Jesus loving the broken, rejected Samaritan woman at the well—and Jesus loving angry, frightened, back-stabbing Peter—and Jesus lovingly embracing and blessing marginalized children of all shapes and sizes. Each of the human beings in these stories was suddenly, wonderfully, and deeply me. I can remember driving down a street in our neighborhood, tears running down my face as I shouted over and over in my empty car, "He loves me! God is my Father, and he loves me!" At one point I almost stopped and got out to embrace a mailman who was trudging house-to-house in the deep, crusty snow. I know it sounds crazy. But when after years and years of emptiness you finally find out that the God of the universe is your Father and he loves you, you feel like you've got to tell someone. And you really want them to know that he loves them too.

One other huge piece of the healing process—the men and women who began to speak and live the Father's love into my heart. A few are pastors, a few are therapists, one is my wife—all are my friends. They each have their own issues and in many ways are on the same journey to experience the

Father's love. But God began to use each of them to show something of his heart toward me as his son. Remember, one of the crucial ways we heal from being unloved is by being loved. And being loved like the Father, in the long run, always trumps the wounds of our earthly fathers.

One such healing moment stands out. My friend Ed and I had just led a weekend retreat together. After everyone else had gone home, we started debriefing the experience, and Ed was trying to encourage me in some way. I wasn't having any of it. My perfectionist-type emptiness was telling him in clear but unspoken ways to back off.

In the next moment, something came over him. He scooted his chair uncomfortably close to mine, put my head in his hands, and brought his face so near I could smell his breath. Then he locked onto my eyes and said, "Kevin, don't you understand? I . . . just . . . love you." I'll never forget it. That very moment a huge glacier-like chunk of satanic lie about being unloved was flushed out of my spiritual veins. Through Ed, I heard the Father say, "Kevin, don't you understand? I . . . just . . . love you." I can still hear those words in my heart from my Abba today.

Listen—my purpose in telling a deeper piece of my story is absolutely not to lay out some kind of gilded path to a seemingly easy healing. There is no such path. There's only a long and dangerous battle with an enemy who is determined to convince each of us that we're not loved and never will be loved, so we might as well live out our miserable empty lives grasping for anything and everything to dull the pain. The reason I am taking the risk to expose my own journey is to encourage you that the battle is worth fighting. And that the battle can be won.

I'm not completely healed. I'm still healing. When I'm not grounded in the Father's love, I promise you that I hear— loud and clear—the beckoning siren voices of the far country of anger, performance, perfectionism, and emptiness. And sometimes I act out. Fourteen years ago I lost my second church, in part because I responded out of emptiness to the stress of shepherding in the body of Christ. A few weeks ago, my youngest daughter gently told me that even as I was healing during her growing-up years, I managed to deeply wound her in some ways that she is still trying to recover from. And last night I argued with Carla because for a brief, disconnected moment I responded out of insecurity when I thought she was rejecting me.

But here is the amazing, encouraging truth for all of us: Even on those days, there is a "magic deeper still"[5]—a truth deeper than emotions and temporary feelings—the truth about my Father's love for me. So even when I journey back to the far country, I don't stay there very long. Sooner than later, I come to my senses and choose to run back home.

Listen carefully: The healing is real. The healing is for you. Our God is a Father who wants to heal your broken heart. Own your emptiness—and if your emptiness is in part connected to your earthly dad, own that too. Bring your pain to your Abba. Ask him to begin to heal you. You don't need to live empty anymore.

A few years ago I asked thirteen young men if they had any interest in hanging out with some other brothers on a regular basis. I told them I thought most men were stuck living as "emotionally immature little boys in grown men's bodies" and that our infantile attitudes, behavior patterns, and baggage were hurting and sometimes destroying those closest to us and keeping us from partnering with Jesus Christ to bring healing to others. I invited them to the intense healing process of revealing the secrets and hidden mess that has kept us from living as full-grown sons of the Father. I promised that if we committed to walk out that kind of intimacy together, God would meet us there in that frightening but freeing honesty.

Twelve men didn't just say "yes" but "heck yes, and when do we start?" On just our second evening together, we opened the New Testament to Ephesians 1:3: "Blessed be the God and Father of our Lord Jesus Christ, who has blessed us in Christ with every spiritual blessing" (ESV). Then I asked the men to talk honestly about their relationships with their earthly fathers—and how that earthly dad relationship impacted their ability to receive the truth of Ephesians 1:3 about how their heavenly Father has loved them and blessed them.

Silence. Followed by more silence. Then, slowly, the young men began to tell their stories.

My father never opened his heart to me about
anything. He was emotionally shut down and
distant. So it's really hard to believe there's a God
who wants to connect with me as a heavenly Father.

My dad left our family when I was young and has never taken an interest in me. But he's known for bedding plenty of women—all the while preaching at his church each Sunday. God as Father? Wow.

Dad was a missionary. He was all about "saving the lost" and loved it when I "helped." But he never really seemed all that interested in me. Does God really want me? Or just a soldier for his cause?

My main memory of my dad is a stern look and correcting voice. I had "done it wrong again." Dad wasn't a bad guy—he just didn't know much about grace. Or affection. Or how to say, "I just love you, son." And now, it's hard to believe God wants those things for me.

I never knew my dad. He left before I could know him. And now he's dead. Having a dad—earthly or heavenly . . . I'm not certain what that's supposed to be like. But I'd sure like to know.

Every man shared. Every man but one cried. That night those twelve brothers began their journey home to a Father who couldn't wait to receive them. The same loving Father who anxiously waits for you.

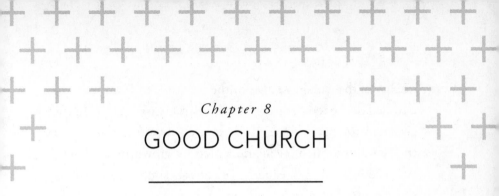

Chapter 8

GOOD CHURCH

If there's trouble, all us freaks have is each other.
ABE SAPIEN, *Hellboy*

We, the many, are one body in Christ.
ROMANS 12:5, BLB

A FEW YEARS AGO, I drove to Chicago for a long weekend to hang out with my daughter Andrea; her husband, Dusty; and, of course, my two-year-old granddaughter, Ada. On Sunday morning Dusty, Andrea, and Ada drove to church while I decided to stay back and hang out with my exhausted self. A couple of hours later, their dog began to bark, the garage door opened, and little Ada strutted happily through the door and proclaimed, "I had good church today, Papa!"

I immediately choked up. At first I wasn't sure why. But then it came to me. It was the loaded phrase "good church" innocently tumbling out of the mouth and heart of a two-year-old. What could little Ada possibly mean by "good church"? She obviously wasn't referring to the pastor's sermon or the quality of the worship music or the way the Lord's Supper was handled or the temperature in the sanctuary or the taste of the coffee in the foyer. Ada's "good church" wasn't about any of the typical points of evaluation used by grown-up believers. Because Ada's church experience consists simply and entirely of riding to the church building with loving parents, walking into a preschool room where she is greeted by a kind and loving Miss Beth, hearing a simple story about a loving Jesus, hanging out with a small group of children her age who may or may not be in loving moods, and having a few crackers and some juice served, well, lovingly. That's what "good church" is to Ada—a goodness she feels so profoundly and deeply that "I had good church today, Papa!" is the first reality bursting from her heart the moment she arrives home.

Loving parents, loving Miss Beth, a loving Jesus, mostly loving young brothers and sisters—could it be that "good church" for Ada is exactly what "good church" is meant to be for all of us? A place where the love of our Abba isn't simply talked about but profoundly experienced in a way that heals us?

In the 1999 Academy Award–winning film *The Green Mile*, John Coffey is an inmate in a 1935 death row Louisiana prison, falsely imprisoned for taking the lives of two little girls. In a tender conversation with Paul Edgecombe, a guard with whom he has become the closest of friends, Coffey says softly,

I'm tired, boss . . . tired of bein' on the road, lonely as a sparrow in the rain. I'm tired of never havin' me a buddy to be with, to tell me where we's going to or comin' from or why. Mostly I'm tired of people bein' ugly to each other. I'm tired of all the pain I feel and hear in the world, every day. They's too much of it. It's like pieces of glass in my head . . . all the time. Can you understand?[6]

Yes, John. We understand. We're all in a battle. It's been going on for a long, long time. It's cosmic. It's spiritual. It's a battle between our Father God who loves us and wants us to live forever—and an enemy who is called Satan, the accuser, the devil, the father of lies, an angel of light who hates us and wants every last one of us eternally dead. And whether we choose to really engage in the battle or not, the battle comes to us—and every one of us gets hurt. Every single day. It's like pieces of glass in our heads, and yes, there's way too much of it. We need healing. Every last one of us needs to be healed.

Enter the obscure rabbi Jesus of Nazareth, who stood up in his home synagogue around 30 AD and read from the prophet Isaiah: "He has sent me to heal the brokenhearted, to proclaim liberty to the captives" (Luke 4:18, JUB). Then he proceeded to walk around Israel for the next three years doing just that: healing the physically, spiritually, and emotionally broken and wounded—Jew and Gentile, male and female, old and young, Pharisees and tax collectors, soldiers and sinners, misfits and murderers, along with the untouchables and the unwanted. He didn't just rework the Torah and preach at the people to do better, do more, and get with the program. Face-to-face with the very worst the enemy could throw at first-century human beings—disease, loneliness, separation, and death—the prophet whom many called King drew near and spoke to them like they mattered, touched them with compassion, and healed each and every one in body and spirit, setting them free.

And then suddenly, the Healer from Nazareth was crucified and gone. But before it all went down, he told his closest followers, "I'm going and you can't go with me. But, in fact, you're going to stay behind—and be me. If you walk with me, if you stay together in me, if you keep your eyes on me and allow my powerful love to saturate your life—from now on you will be the ones who heal the brokenhearted and set the captives free. I am going to continue to heal . . . through you" (John 14:1-3, 15:4-17, author's paraphrase).

Perhaps this is why Paul, over and over, passionately calls Jesus' followers "the body of Christ." We're not just "congregants" or "parishioners"—together we actually are the hands, feet, eyes, voice, and healing touch of Jesus of Nazareth. And perhaps this is why Paul begs us to "love one another" (Romans 13:8) and why he says that frankly, without love, we are absolutely "nothing" (1 Corinthians 13:2) because the one who loves "has fulfilled the law" (Romans 13:8). Love does what the law could never do—it heals us. Remember Peter's words to persecuted, strung out, wounded Jesus followers in first-century Asia Minor: "Above all things have fervent love for one another, for 'love will cover a multitude of sins'" (1 Peter 4:8, NKJV). Maybe he meant, "You're beat up. You're bleeding out. You need respite and healing. And as you—the actual body of Jesus Christ—turn to one another in the power of his love, your Abba will heal you through each other from the death-dealing impact of all kinds of sin." Maybe good church is where broken people meet Jesus—through the loving acts of his people and body—and experience the healing power of the love of God. Maybe anything else isn't "good church." In fact, maybe anything else isn't church at all.

That's what my sister in Christ Elle would say. Invited by a friend, Elle came to us at Hope Community a few years back. By her own admission, when she arrived she was a mess—emotionally, physically, and spiritually. Elle was the seventh of eight children born into a fairly prominent Grosse Pointe family that owned a successful, historic wholesale furniture store in Detroit. Her mom was an emotionally distant woman who made her feel like she was never enough. "I was made fun of," Elle told me. "I couldn't even get sick right. My mom called me a hypochondriac and rarely took me seriously when I said I was ill. Over the years she labeled me as the child who didn't know what she was talking about."

Elle was closer to her dad and felt his love. "My father had integrity," she said. "In his relationship with me, his word was his bond." Unfortunately, her dad was also close friends with Jack Daniels, which created space for a whole lot of chaos in the home. Her parents fought all the time. "There was so much anger," Elle told me. "Shot glasses flying around the room, verbal abuse, and physical violence. As a child I knew something wasn't right—but I also didn't really know anything was wrong. It was just us."

In 1985, at the age of twenty-three, Elle left purgatory and entered a corner of hell. She had been working as a medical assistant at a doctor's office for about three years when one night, on the way home from the job, her car was broadsided and totaled. She wouldn't go to the hospital because she thought her mom would call her paranoid. The result was an untreated closed head injury. From that time on, she was shaky, couldn't focus, and could no longer handle any kind of pressure. For the next several years, she tried to work—first at a hospital, then her original doctor's office, then a dentist's office. "They thought I was a drug addict," she said. "I smoked and drank coffee but had never been into drugs. Except for weed. Weed calmed me down."

After the wreck, things slid downhill at home as well. Later, in 1985, Elle went to her folks late one evening and said, "Forget it. I'm moving out." Her dad replied, "You're screwed up." Elle said, "Well, I might as well be screwed up out there—because I'm not learning anything in here and I ain't gettin' no love." She moved eight times between 1985 and 1991, when she landed a few blocks away from what is now the location of Hope Community Church. After that last move, Elle never worked seriously again, eventually applying for disability. In the years following, the government check became her primary support. For the next couple of decades, she lived sparsely and tried hard to deal with her family, all the while attempting, mostly alone, to slowly heal from the mess of her past. In 2011, she hit another rough patch. She found herself once again choking on shame and feeling rejected and labeled by her family—they now said she had "special needs"—during a period of infighting about money and the family financial legacy. Elle told me much later, "You know, Pastor Kevin, I was born on the opening day of deer season. Sometimes, in those dark days, I thought it would have been better if I had been shot."

And then Elle showed up at Hope, skeptical about church but starving for some kind of authentic human connection. When we sat down a few weeks ago to hear more of her story, this is what she said:

> The day I walked into Hope, I knew I was home.
> Hope has been a place where I can be real, where
> I can have good days and bad days. It reminds me
> of being with my grandparents when I was a little
> girl—I feel safe. People want to actually hear what
> I have to say. My words don't go in one ear and out
> the other. And if you're "off center," folks treat you
> like an adult. You're respected, not belittled or put
> down. In fact, they love you enough to help you
> come back. Pastor Kevin, the love and acceptance of
> me simply being me has helped me heal.

"Good church, Papa." A community filled with folks like Kennell, Brian, Sophia, June, and many others, including my dear friends Lesley, Sue, and Monique—and from distant six-by-six cells, Samson, Lenell, Christopher, and a dozen others. Wounded healers who on any given day may not have much advice or even a ready Bible verse. But what they do have to offer is the deep and powerful and sometimes messy love that is in the process of healing them. It is this love alone that covers a multitude of sins. It is this love that Elle and the rest of us cannot live without. It's not the YouTube-ready worship band or the podcast-quality preaching, the form-fitted programming or the comfortable surroundings. That's all fine, and of course all of it can help us grow in this way or that. But none of these things can in and of themselves heal us. Listen, according to the very apostles of Jesus Christ, even the powerful Word of God—without love—cannot heal us. Only love unleashes the healing. The love of a God who doesn't just love us but is *in love* with us and promises to love us deeply and unconditionally all the way home.

A couple of months ago, Elle went on a trip to see a friend in California. She was gone for two weeks and secretly wondered if anyone would really miss her or if she would return and no one would have even noticed. I get it. She's still healing, and for all of us who wrestle with shame or rejection and have battled to encounter the love we so desperately need, we fear that to be out of sight is to be out of mind. There are so many interesting people and exciting experiences—how can we compete with all of that? There can't possibly be enough love left over for us, especially if we're gone for a while. But when Elle returned, this is what she told me:

> When I got back from California, first it was Pete who said, "Where have you been, Elle? I've missed you." Then I heard everyone saying, "We missed

you. We've learned so much from you." Someone
else asked if I was going to help with the community
garden again. And Dan said, "When you aren't here,
it isn't the same, Elle." I could really see it and feel
it—one more time—that I am noticed, needed,
valued. Elaine told me she even missed the way I
worship. I'm not sure she knows that the only reason
I'm alive is because of God. I finally get it deep in
my heart that he loves me simply because I'm me—
and that's why when I worship, I jump up and down
for joy.

About a year ago, Elle handed me a handwritten note
on lined paper that listed twenty-six different brothers and
sisters in the body of Jesus at Hope who had touched her in
very specific ways.

Kastner for loving me unknowingly . . . Joe for
showing me what true respect is . . . Verlona for
her consistent encouragement . . . James for seeing
that I love all . . . Gabby for always smiling and
acknowledging me . . . Bertha for always asking
me "How's the dog?" . . . Barb for trusting me
to pet sit . . . Marlene for loving me like a big
sister . . . James and Laurie for their kindness
and caring . . . Mark for telling me to trust my
intuition . . . Alberta for saying I'm missed when I'm
gone . . . sister Rita for teaching me when I'm sick to

give it some time. Thank you to all. Kevin, I believe the body of Christ has become a flock. I haven't felt this kind of love and support in a lifetime. It's home.

From secretly wondering if it would have been better to be shot on the day of her birth to jumping up and down in worship because "I finally know God loves me"—Elle's life is living proof that "good church" has the power to heal a broken spirit and fill an empty heart.

+ + +

But how does the healing process in "good church" actually happen? It's clear that God promises his love will heal us, but how? Some might say it doesn't matter "how"—it only matters that the healing is available in and through the body of Christ. Fair enough. But my gut tells me that it might help some of us to know that this process isn't some kind of new-age magic masquerading as the healing power of Jesus. If we knew how and why God's love is able to heal us through "good church," it might encourage us to stop settling for "bad church"—to stop lying to ourselves that a better sermon or better song alone can heal us—to stop simply "talking about the love of God" and to passionately pursue or help shape a community of Jesus followers where his love can actually be experienced.

So, first, what if this healing is most deeply embodied and expressed in the New Testament concept of "fellowship"? For years I—along with countless others—have been convinced that "fellowship" has to mean more than hanging out together around coffee and doughnuts with maybe a little prayer and Bible mixed in. In Acts 2:42, Luke says the earliest believers first "devoted themselves to the apostles' teaching," which makes sense because everything about our life together rests on the truth of Jesus' life, instruction, example, death, and resurrection—along with Israel's history, wisdom, and prophecy that set the stage for his coming. But the apostle's teaching is not listed alone. The second priority of early church life was "fellowship," the rich Greek term *koinonia*, which at its core means "to share in or to participate in together." One way the early believers experienced this "sharing" was through holding their goods and resources "in common" (verse 44). Jesus gave his life for each of them, so it makes sense that they felt compelled to share with one another everything they had. By implication, the same kind of tangible fellowship ought to be available in the church today.

But what if the word *fellowship* also implies the exchange of something even more powerful and foundationally life-giving? John says that the apostles experienced the fellowship of both God the Father and God the Son—and invite each of us as believers into that same fellowship (1 John 1:3). Paul echoes John's thoughts about the fellowship we share with the Son (1 Corinthians 1:9) and adds that we also have the fellowship of the Holy Spirit (2 Corinthians 13:14). If that's true, each of us who believe in Jesus, no matter how wounded or empty we feel at the moment, somehow carry around in our body and spirit the koinonia of the Triune God of the universe!

But what exactly do we "share" with our God in this fellowship that might contribute to our ability to share his healing? John's prologue to his first letter gives the best clue: It's about his *life*! He says this word three times in two verses (1 John 1:1-2). We share the very life of God—life that is not just about eternal quantity but eternal quality. In other words, the "eternal life" that God gives us in fellowship with him includes, of course, the promise of living with him forever. But it also encompasses his eternal quality of life: his character of love, joy, peace, patience, strength, endurance, goodness, justice, courage—and his healing compassion toward his wounded people.

When we authentically turn toward one another in love in the community of faith—when we give our lives through word or action or touch or prayer or simply being fully present with one another—we are "sharing" our healing, loving God's eternal quality of life. We share in fellowship with one another what our God shares in his fellowship with us. This healing fellowship doesn't demand any particular ritual, liturgy, music, or type of worship service—or even any particular spiritual gift or level of personal spirituality. Healing occurs when we simply share the life and love of God with the believer sitting across from us, in whatever form love dictates at the moment. By being truly present to and with one another—out of love—we share the powerful, healing, life-giving presence of our God. And slowly, surely, miraculously, we begin to be healed.

This may be one reason why Jesus says, "Where two or three gather in my name, there am I with them" (Matthew 18:20). And why the author of Hebrews says to a persecuted first-century community of believers, "Don't ever stop coming together" (10:25, author's paraphrase). And why Paul shouts to the dysfunctional, disobedient Corinthian church, "The eye cannot say to the hand, 'I have no need of you'" (1 Corinthians 12:21, NKJV)—because only in relationship, in the body of Christ, can we most profoundly share and unleash the healing power of the fellowship of the life of God.

The profound power of "fellowship" is backed by neurobiological fact. As I mentioned earlier, science tells us that we experience most of our emotional wounding in our limbic brain. These "right brain" wounds are caused by hurt and trauma in relationship and can be felt over the course of a lifetime. But these right brain wounds can be healed: by the power of experiencing the relational opposite of the original wound.[7] Healthy, loving relationship has the power to help heal trauma caused by unhealthy, unloving relationship. The experience of love heals the wounding experience of un-love.

Sometimes you can literally see and feel the healing impact of this kind of "fellowship" in a matter of moments. A few years ago, I was preaching in a church in Wisconsin about—what else?—the love of the Father. At the end of the service, I asked a brother sitting a few rows back to join me in role-playing the beginning of Jewish Sabbath, where the father traditionally speaks a blessing over each of his children. I told the man—who looked to be in his forties, was dressed in business casual, and built like an NFL linebacker—that he would play the role of my son, and for the moment, I would be his dad. He nodded his permission, so I knelt down in front of him, placed my hand around the back of his neck, came close to him, and began to speak a blessing to him.

I told him how blessed I was to be his father, how I remembered so well the very moment of his birth, and how I wept because God had given me a precious little boy. I told him I was proud of him then and so very proud of him now, not primarily because of his accomplishments, but simply because he was himself—and I just loved him. I told him I was glad he played football, but it didn't really matter to me if he scored the winning touchdown or fumbled on the goal line—I was simply proud that he went out and tried. And I told him I loved that he was teachable. And that he loved his mother and sisters well. And that he was compassionate. And I told him I knew that it was tough in the world and he wouldn't always feel safe, but that no matter what, whether he was at the top of his game or struggling, I would always, always be there for him. All he needed to do was look over his shoulder, and—as long as God gave me breath—I would be there. And then I pulled this giant of a forty-five-year-old man close and kissed him on the cheek and whispered, "I love you, son. And I always will."

As I was speaking this blessing, a peaceful stillness came over the eight hundred people in the auditorium. All that could be heard was the quiet shedding of tears as the brothers and sisters in the room allowed the father blessing to take them somewhere deep into their own hearts. But what really moved me was the response of my "son." During the entire blessing, he sat with his huge arms crossed over his chest, not one muscle moving or even twitching, looking me right in the eye—while his own tears rolled down his face. After church, one of the leaders came to me and said, "I just talked to the gentleman who role-played with you, and he told me that this was the first time he has ever been to our church—and actually, due to some religious wounds, the first church he has been to in years. Then he told me something else. He said that what just happened was the most significant moment of his entire life."

That, my friends, is "good church."

So are the words magic? Is it the power of suggestion that seems to so deeply impact others when we simply turn to them in love and give them what we have to offer in Jesus' name? Or could it be the fellowship of our loving God, the profound healing power of "good church" to cover a multitude of sins?

I can't think of a single person in our community of believers who sticks around because of the "typical church" stuff that attracts and holds so many followers of Christ in our culture. They come and engage because they are empty and desperate to know the healing love of God in Jesus. They are tired of just hearing about it and faking their experience of it—they want to intimately know, deeply feel, and live the rest of their lives in that love.

How about you? Are you getting this? It's impossible to

simply read, sing, study, podcast, or educate our way into experiencing the love of Jesus. Human beings simply cannot heal without the shared koinonia of God. In order to heal from the deep wounding of the enemy in our soul, we must connect with other sons and daughters of God who are done playing the game and who want to engage in emotionally, spiritually raw, naked and unashamed fellowship. The exchange of the deep, deep love of Jesus is the only commodity in the universe that can heal us all.

Just ask Nicola. She was born in Yorkshire, England, and moved to Grosse Pointe, Michigan, in 1964 at the age of six. She was raised in a very, very proper English family—which meant Nicola was very, very different from her six-year-old Michigan friends. She wore different clothes and different shoes and spoke with a very different accent.

Did you catch that key word? *Different*. In other words, alone.

By age fourteen, academically brilliant but bored and with very few friends, Nicola started to drink. She would drink not only in Michigan but would go home to England in the summer and drink cider with her friends and shandies at the pubs. Nevertheless, after graduating high school, she was accepted at the University of Michigan. And one afternoon while walking to class as a nineteen-year-old freshman, she was hit by a car. Nicola was unconscious for fourteen days, in the hospital for twenty-one days—and then began a life of struggle that lasted the next twenty years.

Nicola tried to stay at U of M but finally gave up in 1980.

She started using cocaine after the accident and overdosed—flatlined—twice in the next decade. She had a couple of kids and had been married a couple of times. Both husbands abandoned her at crucial moments during those difficult years. She met her second husband at culinary school in England. He used her to get to the United States and divorced her right after their daughter was born.

In 1988, Nicola received a grant to start a catering business. She was even written up in the *Ann Arbor News*: "Single Mom Creates Business!" Shortly thereafter Nicola met a six-foot-nine bouncer in a bar—who got busted for drugs and went to prison. Nicola married him in a prison ceremony. "We used to party together," Nicola said, "but I loved him and really tried to make the marriage work."

On July 25, 1996, on the way to a final meeting about a wedding she was catering, her car flipped on M-14 and Beck Road. Nicola was thrown to the other side of the freeway and woke up in the U of M hospital. She was released after thirty days but spent the next four months in a hospital bed at home. She had broken her pelvis in four places and sustained a closed head injury.

After this second accident, she lost her business—and started losing track of time. She also lost any kind of ability to stand for a long while—a necessity in the food-service business. And she lost her husband. He received parole, cheated on her, dropped dirty, went back to prison, and then asked for a divorce because, Nicola said, "He couldn't face having to take care of me." She lost her home and began living on the street, sleeping on porches. She also lost her freedom. She was arrested and spent a few weeks in the Washtenaw County Jail. The key word during this second long and difficult period of Nicola's life? *Loss.*

After her release, Michigan Rehab Services helped her get back into community college for culinary arts to hone and refine her skills and get her ready to work again. She graduated with honors. Amazingly, in 2001, Nicola secured a mortgage and moved to an extremely "challenged" house, where she lives today—just a few blocks down from Hope Community Church. She worked at a café six days a week—until her car broke down. Then another car got stolen and another got into an accident. Soon after she had only a bike to ride, kitchen work was nonexistent, and quite frankly Nicola was sad, tired, drinking a fair amount, struggling with Hepatitis B, and simply trying to survive.

And then, at this low point, her life began to change.

I found Hope—and found hope. I didn't know anything about Jesus. God, maybe, but Jesus had never been explained to me. I didn't know what he did for me. The fact that he loved me enough to die for me and forgive all of my sins. That kind of love has helped me finally start to love myself. Hope didn't just tell me about that love—Hope has shown me that love. I've never been judged at Hope for what I had been before. I felt forgiven not only by God but by the people. Even when I came to church after a bout with drinking, arms were open. I was encouraged to get back into recovery and was never judged. I used to feel so unworthy—but now I know I am worthy.

Secured by the love of God in Jesus Christ over a period of years, Nicola's gifted, passionate self finally has a solid foundation from which to be unleashed. Love sets us free to be exactly who God created us to be. Nicola is now known for, among other things, organizing our community garden. In the summer, there are always fresh vegetables for anyone who needs them. Nicola also works tirelessly as a community activist, attending block club meetings and urban garden trainings and keeping her ears and heart open for anyone who might be struggling to find their way—as she struggled herself for so many years. She still dreams about having a community center kitchen to not only feed people but serve as a place where folks on the block can come and be together. Nicola plans for the kitchen itself to be in a garage next to her house, a garage that right now doesn't have a roof. I just love it.

Nicola's journey isn't perfect. "When I'm too tired, I'm still tempted to drink," she said. Like me, she isn't healed—she's healing. When we sat together the other day she said, "Pastor Kevin, I get up every morning and journal, and the opening line is always, always, 'Thank you, Lord, for this day . . .'" Then she told me about how she had just received a beautification grant for her block club—a check for three thousand dollars. She gave me a hug and whispered, "I wrote the grant completely on my own."

As she was getting ready to leave my office, she said to me, "Pastor Kevin, the world will continue to slap me in my face. But it's okay because Hope has shown me that I am loved, and my heart is healing."

And at that moment, all I could hear in my head was little Ada shouting to me, "I had good church today, Papa." Indeed.

Chapter 9

FORGIVEN

Breathe the free air again, my friend.
GANDALF TO THEODEN, KING OF ROHAN,
The Two Towers

But God . . . because of the great love with which he loved us,
even when we were dead in trespasses, made us alive
together with Christ.
PAUL, EPHESIANS 2:4-5, ESV

I CAN REMEMBER sitting in a courtroom in the early '90s, awaiting the judge's verdict. I wasn't on trial, but a friend of mine was. He was a drug dealer who had put his faith in Jesus at a men's retreat just a few months back. But he got busted—ironically, on the way home from the retreat—for a drug deal he had made just days before he met God. The amount of cocaine he sold demanded a harsh and lengthy sentence. The defense attorney appealed passionately to both judge and jury about my friend's newfound spiritual life and the fact that he wasn't a violent man—but to no avail. I'll be haunted forever by the sound of the judge's gavel and his booming voice pronouncing the sentence over my friend. Guilty as charged.

Unforgiven.

Outside of its diabolical partner, shame, feeling unforgiven might be the greatest emotional barrier between us and our experience of the Father's love. Remember, shame is connected to "who we are" and is in itself a deep hindrance to believing we are loved. But closely related—based not so much in who we are but "what we do"—is the core longing for forgiveness. For someone in ultimate authority to say to us, "That thing you did that was wrong—that crime you committed, those wounding words, that self-centered behavior, that decade or two of acting out and all the people you hurt so profoundly—all that moral debt has been wiped clean from the ledger of your life. You are no longer found guilty. You are forgiven."

We struggle to believe in forgiveness. What kind of chaos would reign if there were no consequences for wrongdoing? After all, if someone hurts us or our friends or loved ones, we want them to pay. There's a saying in the neighborhood: "You do the crime, you do the time." So it's counterintuitive for us to believe that we can be let off, that the stink and stain of our sinful actions against others and against God can somehow be wiped clean.

But even with all our doubts about forgiveness, we long to be forgiven! I think most of us understand that forgiveness doesn't mean that what we've done doesn't matter or that it wasn't wrong or that there aren't human repercussions or that we don't wish we wouldn't have messed up in the first place. We get all of that. What we long for is to be able to look our God in the face and for once, just once, feel like he doesn't see a lifetime of screw-ups. We don't even blame God for turning away from us in disgust because if we stared at the sinful baggage dripping from every part of our being, we would turn away too. But we long for it to not be so. We long to be forgiven because we sense that if we aren't forgiven, we can't be loved. We're so afraid it's impossible to be both forgiven and loved—by God.

But what if God does forgive us and also loves us? In fact, what if God doesn't forgive us first and then love us—but instead his love for us moves him to forgive us. A few years ago, I listened to a young artist named Maude Maggart sing Irving Berlin's love song "How Deep Is the Ocean." When I first heard the lyrics, I was stunned. Of course, the song itself is about the love between two people. But I couldn't help thinking that behind all great love songs is the deep, costly, pursuing love of God. In *The Magician's Nephew*, C. S. Lewis depicts Aslan singing at the dawn of Narnia—a song "beyond comparison, the most beautiful . . . ever heard."[8] Imagine God singing the following words to Adam and Eve right after their willful, defiant betrayal, when they so desperately needed mercy and forgiveness:

How much do I love you? I'll tell you no lie.
How deep is the ocean? How high is the sky? . . .
And if I ever lost you, how much would I cry. [9]

Then, what if God sang, "I'll tell you how much I would cry—my tears over losing you would fill an ocean, they would reach to the sky." I can hear some of us now. "Okay, God loves me—but not like that. If I don't perform, if I screw up, if it becomes inconvenient, if I don't jump through all the religious hoops, God's love for me won't last."

The phrase "God loves you" has become so dumbed down or maybe just so theologically sterile that we can't imagine him loving us with any emotion, passion, or longing. If any of my three daughters ever need me, I'll do whatever it takes to be with them. And my greatest fear as a dad is losing one of them—the issue wouldn't be how much I would cry but whether I could ever stop. I'm just an earthly father with unhealed wounds, baggage, and issues, and I love my girls with that kind of passion, emotion, and longing. Yet we struggle to believe that our eternal Abba, who says "I am love" (1 John 4:8), could love us even remotely like that. No wonder we find it hard to believe he could ever forgive us.

Yet Paul says exactly that: "God, who is rich in mercy, because of His great love with which He loved us, even when we were dead in trespasses, made us alive together with Christ (by grace you have been saved)," (Ephesians 2:4-5, NKJV). In other words, our God loves us more than enough to forgive us. His love and mercy trump our deadness in sin—even the sin you're thinking of right now that you've convinced yourself is unforgiveable.

But the core, ancient New Testament message of forgiveness is not that God's magnificent love moved him to some kind of "sentimental bypass" of our sin. He didn't simply sweep our rebellion under a thick cosmic carpet so we could all pretend it didn't exist. Instead, his all-encompassing love moved him to sacrificial action. He sent Jesus, the one he called "beloved Son," to a death by crucifixion—a death "for us." He didn't just die as an unfortunate victim of a combination of Jewish and Roman injustice—he willfully died for the sins of everyone, everywhere, for all time. He died where we should have died and paid a penalty we should have paid. For those of us who struggle to believe we can be forgiven because "someone has to pay for my sin," God says, "Yes, justice says someone must pay. And Someone has. My Son, Jesus—because he loves you." And then, three days later, that same Jesus rose from the dead to prove—as one of my preacher friends in Detroit likes to say—that the check cleared.

Sin's penalty satisfied. Death swallowed up by life. Guilt overwhelmed by forgiveness. That's the deeper truth we want to believe—that we long to believe. But the struggle is to break through the barriers of wound and shame in our hearts so we can receive it. If just recounting the redemptive historical events of Jesus' life and explaining New Testament forgiveness theology was enough, then most of us would without doubt believe in our forgiveness already. But we need more. We need to feel this truth. We need to experience it.

If I could, I would reach through the pages of this book right now and gently take your head in my hands, look you in the eye, and tell you I love you—hoping that my stumbling attempt to help you experience unconditional love might help you feel the very love and forgiveness of God himself.

Of course, I can't do any of that. But there's something I can do. I can tell you Cindy Carter's story.

Cindy was born in 1945 in Manhattan, New York, and then moved to Los Angeles with her mother and father when she was a toddler. Her mom was a believer in Jesus, so Cindy not only felt close to her but had the privilege of attending a Catholic parish school. But her dad was an alcoholic, and his emotional baggage and abusive behavior controlled the home. He was mean. He beat her mother. When Cindy stepped in to defend her mom, he beat her too. Yet Cindy told me, "I still loved him." Then, when she was ten years old, everything changed. Her own dad—the man God trusted to take care of this little girl—flipped God off, violated and violently took advantage of her, and raped her.

When Cindy told me this part of her story, I didn't know whether to weep or swear or take a hammer to a wall. I wanted to start hunting for Satan on the spot—to take him out—as if he was simply some kind of frothing, insane animal who had to be dealt with before he killed again. As for Cindy, her eyes filled with tears and turned toward the ground, and her sixty-nine-year-old voice choked as her heart broke one more time.

Cindy told me that after the rape her dad went to jail, and soon after, inexplicably, her mom bailed him out. When he came home, her mom asked him if he wanted a drink. She then went into the kitchen for a meat cleaver and a butcher knife. When her mom came back out of the kitchen, she tried to kill him. But the trauma and stress of everything caused her to stroke right on the spot. The ambulance came, and after a series of tests, Cindy's mom found out she had a malignant brain tumor. She made Cindy promise not to let them leave her in the hospital to die. So for the next five years, Cindy took care of her mom as she lay in a hospital bed in their home in Los Angeles. Her dad went back to prison immediately after her mom's stroke. But the enemy wasn't done with Cindy. He's never done trying to destroy us. The doctors innocently showed her how to give her mom her pain meds—the powerful, heroin-like Demerol and morphine. One day Cindy said, "Momma, these drugs make you feel better. They're gonna make me feel better too." And they did.

For the next half-decade, Cindy and her mother numbed their very different kinds of pain with prescription medications. That's when Cindy's forty-year heroin habit began. Cindy never had any kind of counseling to help her grieve and heal from what happened to her. All she knew was the pain, and she simply wanted it to stop. When her mom died after five years of cancer treatment, her dad got a prison pass to come to the funeral. He never made it. Instead, he stole the police car that was transporting him to the funeral service, eluded the other officers, and drove off a five-hundred-foot cliff—while fifteen-year-old Cindy watched. She told me, "I buried my mom and dad on the same day. But obviously, there was no funeral for my dad."

Cindy was a minor, so after the funeral, the authorities tried to put her in foster care. But she ran away and hitchhiked to Mexico—some guy in LA told her the best heroin was south of the border. There, at fifteen, she got connected to the Mexican Mafia, who hired her as a "mule" for the next three years. "Pastor," she told me, "I got on and off airplane after airplane with suitcases full of drugs that I was delivering to cities all over the country. I always got paid under the table—and the Mexican dons paid me well. I had everything I needed. When I look back and think about how young I was and what danger I was in, I realize God has had his hand on me all along."

By 1964, Cindy was back in California and involved with Charles Manson and his crew. She said that at the beginning, Manson was all about "peace," but then the drugs happened—LSD, mescaline, and of course, heroin. Cindy remembers the day that a high, whacked-out Manson came to the group and asked them to go kill Sharon Tate. She said, "Heck no. I'm out." Another moment of grace. She soberly shared with me, "I know now what I couldn't know then—all this time I was really looking for the love of Jesus."

Eventually, a ridiculous coastal earthquake frightened her so badly that she impulsively got on an airplane and flew to Arizona, where she didn't know anyone. For the next ten years, Cindy roamed the country. She had begun selling her body for drugs in LA—another death-dealing beginning, another piece of the enemy's strategy to take her out. Cindy told me, "What my dad did to me distorted my under-standing of love. So I just did what I had to do to survive."

Finally, Cindy landed in Detroit, where she exchanged sex

for drugs for the next three decades, mostly in the infamous Cass Corridor. She started as a dancer and then became the manager at the Studio of Living Art, a front for prostitution. There Cindy met a man who took care of her for a time—he gave her shelter and food and supplied her with drugs, of course, in exchange for sex. They had a son together, a son whom Cindy deeply loves and yet rarely sees, which is to this day one of the greatest hurts of her life.

Eventually Cindy landed on the streets with the nickname Tippy Toes and a reputation for being good at what she did. She was also known to have a heart for those who were in tougher shape than she was. "You couldn't walk past someone on the streets hurting worse than you without giving them some money for food," she told me. Night after night for several decades, Cindy took her miniskirt, high heels, and broken heart into the arms of empty, broken men, slowly wasting away. Sometimes death got right up in Cindy's face. One night she opened the door of a car to turn a trick with a guy who had just been ripped off by one of the other girls. He was so angry he shot Cindy—she has a huge, mummy-like scar on her left arm to this day.

Finally, in February 2003, after several decades in the Corridor, with a body "used up" from heroin-filled needles and a spirit that was sucked dry of any kind of real life—Cindy was done.

I went to a hotel where I knew the owners and asked them to lock me in one of the rooms for three days so I could detox and get clean. I got on my knees at the beginning of my stay in that room and cried out to God because I knew if he didn't help me, I was going to die. I had been shooting over two hundred dollars of heroin a day. That's a lot, and I was a mess. The withdrawals were horrible beyond description. After the three days in the room, I went back to the NSO warming center, and they said, "Tippy Toes, we've got to get you to the hospital!" I had bruises all over my body from banging myself against the walls during my withdrawal, and I was dehydrated from vomiting and diarrhea. They told me I was in real dangerous shape.

The ambulance came and took her to Detroit Receiving for a few days until she was well enough. Eventually she ended up at Genesis III—the same treatment center where June Walker landed a few years later. It was there that Cindy, like June, believed in Jesus. The woman who shared Jesus with Cindy was a caseworker named Yolanda Hall. "Everyone told Yolanda not to go near me," Cindy told me. "They said I was crazy!" Obviously, Yolanda didn't listen. When she told Cindy that Jesus Christ loved her so much he died not only to heal her pain but forgive all her sin, the broken little girl in Cindy's fifty-seven-year-old body and spirit couldn't believe in Jesus fast enough! Could it be true? Forty years of the guilt and shame of heroin abuse and prostitution, decades of desperately doing the unspeakable, trying to survive until she was almost dead—wiped clean? Forgiven? Like the woman at the well in John 4, Cindy gulped down the loving, forgiving Jesus, and living water began to hydrate and heal every parched and wounded place in her heart. That's what the real Jesus does.

Are you tracking with Cindy's story? Are you hearing it for real? Cindy did it all—over and over and over again. So much pain. So much failure. So much guilt. So little hope for forgiveness. From anyone. "Christianity" might not have forgiven her. Certain believers in Jesus might never forgive her. Some imposter Jesus might have frightened her with his churchy, misquoted, manipulative words about judgment. But the real Jesus, the One who forgave the wounded prostitute in Luke 7 and the no-name murderer in Luke 23 and the betrayer Peter in John 21—*that* Jesus loved Cindy and forgave Cindy for everything. Could it be that no matter what you have done, the real Jesus truly loves you and is ready to forgive you? Could it be that he's already forgiven you, and it's simply time for you to choose to receive it?

Look, I know there are times when this seems almost impossible. Even as I write these words I'm struggling with an attitude that I thought I was healed from but that has come back in the last few months with a bitter, pervasive vengeance. I'm wondering if Jesus isn't just sick and tired of dealing with me and this thought pattern that I have confessed to him over and over and over again. Could he really love me enough to forgive me one more time, even though I'm struggling to let go of the attitude and have no idea how many more times in the next few days or weeks I will need to confess it again?

The truth about the forgiveness of the real Jesus is something all of us have to live into over and over. He meets us in each situation with the same sacrificial wounds in his hands and side and the same deep love that wipes us clean. That's for sure what Cindy believes. She told me, "Pastor, this is the reason Jesus is my best friend. He always listens to me. He always accepts me. He never judges me. And he always, always forgives me."

The love and forgiveness of Jesus that Cindy received that day at Genesis III began to heal her in ways that can only be described as miraculous. Cindy has been clean for twelve years—never once relapsing. She told me, "Pastor, I'm turning seventy soon, and these have been the best twelve years of my life."

God also restored Cindy's mind. That "crazy" diagnosis wasn't just a reaction from some impatient staff member at Genesis III—it was clinical. They told Cindy she was not only ADHD, but also bipolar and schizophrenic. But after meeting Jesus, no longer. When Cindy was telling me about her diagnosis before she met Jesus in contrast to who she is today, she leaned forward in her chair, and with a look of deeply thankful, spiritual intensity, she said, "Pastor, the power of God can heal us all!" I thought, *This is how the Samaritan woman in John 4:29 must have looked and sounded when she ran back to her hometown and shouted, "Come, see a man . . . "*—a man she truly believed had just saved her life.

One of our pastors, Pam, met Cindy at Genesis III in 2004. Pam brought Cindy to Hope, and a few months later I baptized her. Cindy has been with us ever since. She works in our food pantry, simply walking around and asking people if she can pray for them. Then she takes their hands and bows her head and prays that God would take care of them the same way he has taken care of her.

And you know what else she does? With a few friends who feel the same call, she regularly goes back to the streets she used to walk, bringing the reality of the love and forgiveness of Jesus with her. When they pull up to a corner and the girls come over to the car, Cindy rolls down the window and sticks her mummified, heroin-needle-scarred arms through the window, offering a sandwich and a gift bag full of fresh toiletries. And with hands open wide she says, "Can I pray with you? Do you know how much I love you? Do you know how much Jesus loves you? Do you know he forgave me and now I'm free? And he has already forgiven you, too."

Remember my drug-dealing friend at the beginning of this chapter? The sound of the gavel. Guilty. Unforgiven. Cindy's story shouts something radically different.

When Cindy came off the streets, she had several outstanding warrants that could have immediately put her in jail. But she was fortunate enough to get in a program that meant, if she stayed clean and out of trouble for a certain amount of time, her record would be expunged. A retired pastor from Hope, John Whitfield, took Cindy to every appointment with her probation officer and the judge, twice a month for fifteen months. She never missed. Finally, it was graduation day. Twenty of us from Hope Community sat up in the balcony at 36th District Court to support Cindy. As we watched, many other program participants marched one by one to the middle of the courtroom and faced the judge, who read their case number—and then declared them free.

When Cindy's name was called, she gingerly stepped forward. The judge began to read: "Case #U833383 for Disorderly Conduct and Flagging." There was a pregnant pause. The audience expected the judge to do what she had done for all the other participants, declaring the case closed and Cindy's record expunged and clean.

But the judge wasn't done. She continued to read: "Case #U937800, Case #U952988, Case #U962018, Case #U968328." The room fell silent under the thick heaviness of each number representing one more crime, one more wrongdoing, one more punishable offense.

"Case #U921380, Case #U016966, Case #U864263, Case #U962733, Case #U971110."

Finally, mercifully, the judge stopped. Another long pause. Even the judge herself seemed stunned and deeply moved by the weight of what she had just spoken. None of us sitting in the courtroom knew what came next, because this was different. All the other participants had one number, representing only one crime, one ticket, one offense against society—but Cindy had ten. It felt like there was simply too much to expunge, too much to release, too much to forgive.

And then the judge's voice invaded the overwhelming

atmosphere with authority and conviction: "All cases dismissed. Cindy Carter, you are free to go." Her gavel came down—and the courtroom erupted! Even the judge and court officials were clapping and shouting. Everyone was so happy for Cindy. Of course!

But sitting there in that profound moment on that special day, I sensed that maybe, just maybe, many of us were cheering passionately because we felt like we were seeing "through a glass darkly" a picture of something much more profound than the forgiveness of Detroit's 36th District Court. Maybe we were catching a sacred glimpse of a cosmic courtroom, where some two thousand years ago, the Son of God offered his perfect Self as a sacrifice for our sin. And when he did, the Judge of all the earth—who knew about our dozens and hundreds and hundreds of thousands of sins against his holy character—declared each of us "free." It's the same cosmic courtroom that Paul envisioned in perhaps the greatest statement about the love and forgiveness of our God ever written:

> Who shall bring any charge against God's elect? It is
> God who justifies. Who is to condemn? Christ Jesus
> is the one who died—and more than that, who was
> raised . . . .Who shall separate us from the love of Christ?
> ROMANS 8:33-35, ESV

Paul, the murderer, believed that because of the sacrifice of Jesus, he was no longer condemned—but fully forgiven. A sacrifice motivated by a love that could not envision letting us go. Even when we sin after we believe, we remain judi-cially pardoned—nothing can sever us from the love of the Judge who sees us and our sin through the death of our lover Christ.

But what about the sin we struggle with after we believe in Jesus? Does it matter? Of course. That's why another of Jesus' followers, John, who surely wrestled with his own baggage, writes, "The blood of God's Son Jesus continues to cleanse us from all sin—if we confess our sin, God is faithful and just to forgive us our sin and to cleanse us from all unrighteousness" (1 John 1:7, 9, author's paraphrase).

Sin matters because even though it cannot ever again sever the relationship itself, it can interrupt the intimacy of our relationship with God—because God is light, and he can't be intimate with darkness. But even in the interruption, all we need to do is choose. Again and again. Choose to simply run to him and say, "You're right. I was wrong. I'm back." With authentic confession of sin—no matter what the sin or how many times we have repeated it—we are immediately forgiven, the slate wiped clean and intimacy restored through the blood of Christ.

This is the real Jesus. It's time for us to leave behind the caricature Jesus that the enemy has downloaded into our spirit through years of Pharisaical Bible studies, finger-pointing Christian friends, and bad teaching from the legal-istic and wounded individuals in our lives. The real Jesus looks down from a cross, our sin upon his shoulders, and says with compassion, "Father, forgive them, because they really,

really don't know what they're doing." If you listen carefully, you might even hear him singing from before time began, "And if I ever lost you, how much would I cry? How deep is the ocean, how high is the sky." My guilt-ridden brother or sister—it's time. Let the real, loving, forgiving Jesus bring you home.

Chapter 10

DEEPER THAN FEELINGS

Is the Lord at hand indeed? Many of us have believed in him for a
long time, have also hungered to believe in him when with part of
ourselves we sometimes couldn't believe in much of anything . . . .
Is it finally true what we have believed and hungered to believe?
This side of Paradise, who can say with absolute certainty?
Even Jesus on His cross asked that hardest of questions.
FREDRICK BUECHNER, *Telling Secrets*

Therefore we do not lose heart. Even though our outward man
is perishing, yet the inward man is being renewed day by day.
PAUL, 2 CORINTHIANS 4:16, NKJV

AUDREY BRENNAN IS MY FRIEND. I have known her for twenty-
seven years. She is brilliant and incredibly creative, even working as an interior designer for several years. She has been my
friend Kevin's wonderful wife for thirty-three years and the
mother of three amazing, gifted grown-up kids. Audrey loves
to read, loves to watch *Law & Order*, loves flowers and gardens,
and loves to laugh. And she's a fantastic cook (although she
cooks mostly weird, exotic stuff that is really healthy and that
I refuse to eat). Audrey is also a no-nonsense, serious follower
of Jesus, sacrificially using her gifts in the body of Christ and

loving all kinds of folks deeply and well through lots of mess. In fact, if Audrey and Kevin hadn't opened up their home the week after some hurtful and divisive drama in our last church, Hope Community might not exist today.

And one more thing about my friend Audrey: She has severe, degenerative, debilitating Multiple Sclerosis, the kind that has gotten bad enough over the last eighteen years that she struggles not to be terrified about what is coming next.

Audrey and I have discussed, wrestled with, and lived into the love of God for years, coming to the same conclusion that according to the Scripture and especially according to Jesus, his love is literally everything. So when I asked her to read a few chapters of this book, I couldn't wait to hear what she had to say.

When she finally responded, I was taken back by her reply: "Good stories, true stories, powerful stories—but too neatly packaged and not nearly messy enough to touch me in the reality I'm forced to live into every day." I immediately thought, rather defensively, *Are you kidding me?* But for once, instead of reacting, I pressed in and asked her to tell me more. She said, "Frankly, Kevin, I want to hear more about the struggle to know God and his love when life isn't getting better after we meet him—but is actually constantly and increasingly falling apart. There are many of us who wake up in living hell every day and are challenged to move forward with absolutely no end in sight. What do we do? How do I know God is my good Father and loves me—when my body is shutting down a little more each moment, I'm crying out to him for help, and I hear a whole lot of nothing in response?"

Paul promises God's love will "[fill] us with all [his] full-ness" (Ephesians 3:19, ESV), but what does that mean for someone like Audrey who has to fight to experience that love even while her body betrays her? Audrey's story is for those of us who struggle with a gaping wound or piece of deep hurt that steals hope and tries to crush any experience of the love of God as it shouts, "You'll never be rid of me! I'll be with you every moment for the rest of your life!"

We're sick of canned spiritual answers given to us by folks who can't possibly know the chronic torment we experience in our bodies and hearts and yet try to tell us how we ought to feel. We've cried in front of many therapists, read a boat-load of books, been anointed by this healer and that pastor and another well-meaning group of elders—and truth be told, we've felt so little healing, so little love, that we struggle to pray, struggle to sing, and are desperate to know what to do next. And we don't know who to talk to because even many of our believing friends don't understand and are really frustrated with our fight with chronic pain and doubt.

And Audrey's story isn't just for some elite, suffering few. It's for any of us honest enough to say that at some point in our lives the spiritual battle with the forces of darkness nailed us in the deep core of our body, mind, and spirit. And somewhere along the line, the pain began to feel so absolutely overwhelming and unhealable that we started to lose hope.

Many of us sincerely believe in Jesus Christ and at least in the concept of his love for us, yet we also live with scream-ing doubt-filled questions: Does my particular brand of

pain—and the lack of answers or any type of long-term comfort or prospect of hope—prove that I don't really count?
Can God and his great love be real and present to us in
long-term suffering? Can we know somewhere deeper than
feelings, deeper than circumstantial data, deeper than our
present experience that truly nothing can separate us from
the love of God—even when we're shouting, "My God, my
God, why have you forsaken me?" (Matthew 27:46).

These are the questions Audrey wrestles with every day.
Wrestling with the God who says he loves her but seems to
have abandoned her in pain is, at this point, the key theme
of Audrey's life.

Audrey first believed in Jesus at the age of eight in one of
those old-school, "walk down the aisle" church moments. By
1983, Audrey was a college graduate, married to Kevin, who
was working as a youth pastor in a local church, and living
in an eastern suburb of Detroit. The next fifteen years were
good but not without significant struggle. Kevin and Audrey
faced some deep conflict in their marriage head-on with faith
and grit, and then a few years later courageously held their
youngest, Rachel, while she fought a life-threatening brain
tumor. By that time, the Brennans had become young leaders
in our former church, and by the mid-nineties, Audrey had
joined our staff team. In 1997, at the age of thirty-seven, she
experienced her first clearly diagnosable symptom of Multiple
Sclerosis—a bout with optic neuritis, an inflammation of the
optic nerve that causes blurred vision and often even pain.

Audrey calls this period "the years of absolute denial"

because her inflamed eye calmed down quickly with steroids, and she had no other symptoms. She started working out with a trainer, lost some weight, was feeling great physically, and was on track spiritually. "I didn't do anything MS related for five years," she told me.

Then in 2001, our church blew up, and Audrey believes the deep, relational pain of the split took its toll. MS is an autoimmune disease and is affected by stress. "I remember being so brokenhearted," Audrey said. "Even now I think of the carnage, the broken friendships. How many people don't even go to church today because of all that mess." I suspect that a piece of her continued pain is knowing that the community intended to be the very safest place on earth—the body of Christ—is the place that likely helped kick-start her descent into the hell her disease has become.

In 2002, shortly after the church split, other symptoms began to show themselves. She remembers being in Hawaii with her extended family: "I was down at the beach and had to walk back up a shallow hill and almost couldn't make it because my legs were so dead. At that very moment, I thought—*it begins*." Then she mentions about her twenty-fifth high school reunion in 2003, "You know how everyone stands around and talks? I only had a Diet Coke, and after standing for a while chatting with old friends, I went to take a step, and my legs gave out. I went down like a sack of bricks. I never recovered from that. Twelve years later and my legs haven't been the same."

As she shared her story with me, Audrey paused at this

point. She began to reflect on her illness and how it has impacted her relationship with God, almost as if she couldn't say another word about MS until she brought the elephant in the room—God—into the discussion. As I listened to Audrey talk, weep, and agonize about God and her ongoing pain, I realized anew that sometimes God meets us most profoundly in a place where we have no answers, a place where we have only raw, mysterious, unexplainable God and our best attempt to see him.

Audrey began,

From the very beginning, people have said, "Hey, don't you ever ask God, 'Why me?'" And honestly, I've always had the mentality, "Why not me?" I get it. We live in a fallen, broken world, and bad stuff, horrifying stuff happens to all of us. God didn't cause my MS. Satan is the author of evil and pain, and we're in a spiritual battle, so why not me? Besides, if God ever answered my "why me" question, I guarantee you I wouldn't be satisfied with his answer. What possible reasoning, even from God, would make me say, "Oh, now I understand why you allowed me to get an illness that slowly steals everything from me but my ability to breathe." So, from the very beginning, I've never really been angry at God.

As Audrey was talking, I got the impression that this theology had served her well for a number of years—but that she was getting ready to tell me why that same theology wasn't serving her so well anymore. Finally she said, "I also never thought it would get this bad." And her voice broke.

At that moment, contemplating just how awful it had gotten, I was afraid of asking Audrey questions that might seem too personal—like what happens when she loses her ability to get in and out of the bathroom, and how does she feel about folks she doesn't know invading her home to care for her, and how is the marriage really going, and are your friends standing beside you, and how are your kids responding? I got so nervous that I stammered and stumbled for a moment or two in our conversation. And I realized she has these and a thousand other questions bombarding her every day.

After Audrey collected herself, she went on:

I'm really good at seeing things the way they are going to be—not so good at seeing things as they actually are. But today I get how things are more than ever, because I can no longer escape my reality even for a second. I must deal with my inner journey where I wrestle with my thoughts of God and how he feels about me because I have very little outer life left. I must wrestle with God's love for me. It's the only way I can survive.

Then she said something that cut into my heart: "I think I get angrier at God for how this impacts my family than anything. I don't want them to hurt because I hurt or for their lives to be slowed down or negatively impacted." And my friend cried some more. This time she didn't cry alone.

Some days in the last twelve years of decline, Audrey thought God might heal her. She believes God can heal folks, and so does our church. One night a group from Hope and a few other believing friends came to her house to anoint her and pray for healing. Audrey vividly remembers what happened next:

> A well-meaning someone began praying caveats over what happens if I didn't get healed, and I said in my mind, "You can leave!" After the praying was done and I was still stuck in my chair, I said, "Am I the only one in the room who thinks I should be getting up and walking right now?" No one said a word. The disappointment I felt at not being healed was devastating.

Over the years, folks have tended to say some not-so-helpful things to Audrey like, "God heals us in different ways" or "You'll be perfectly healed when you meet Jesus." We need to take notice and learn a different way if we really desire to be healing agents of the love of God for folks with unexplainable, relentless wounds. As Audrey told me,

> I don't want to hear people's excuses for why God isn't physically healing me right now. I don't feel like God needs excuses. I don't think God needs them to

help fix this for me. And I definitely don't need them to give me vision for what my life will be or might be. I need to feel like they're really with me in the life that I live right now. Be your normal self with me. Tell me about your good day or your bad day. Because that's what normal people do when they're together.

Finally, I gulped and asked her the most difficult question of all: "Audrey, with things where they are, after years of praying and no apparent answer and no assurance things are going to get better and quite possibly could get worse—do you believe that God loves you?" Her response surprised me:

Even though my dad was emotionally silent, I never doubted his love for me as a kid. So when the whole "God's love" thing comes up, even though God, too, seems emotionally silent, I don't really doubt his love either. What I do doubt is that he's even there to begin with. I doubt that he's there more than I ever did. Yet I have seen God in my life—the healing of my marriage and Rachel's tumors—so even now doubt isn't my total reality. But some days I do wake up and wonder if I'm praying to the ceiling. On my good days, I believe he is here, I don't feel singled out, and the MS doesn't cause me to doubt his love for me. On my bad days, I'm pretty sure everything's a joke.

"Maybe it's easier to believe in no God sometimes than to believe that there's a God who says he loves you but then sits and watches you get worse," I said. "When I think of God, I think of hope. When I lose hope, I lose God."

She quickly replied, "Yeah, that's it." And the tears came one more time.

We sat together in silence for a while and then began to talk about people trying to find hope, wondering if they can have a relationship with a loving God when their foundational reality feels so . . . unloving. So I asked her, "Audrey, bottom line, what do you want those folks to hear from you?" She replied in one long stream of intensely personal, foundational truth:

> My reality is that I go back and forth. I have moments—even longer than moments—when I have no hope in my situation. But even on my worst days with MS, I can't deny that I have seen the love of God. And in my doubts, like Thomas, I try to stay close to other followers of Jesus, and I cry out to him and tell him all about how I feel about him, about my doubt, anger, questions, and everything. I ask him to give me eyes to see him, to know his love, even in my pain. And then, somehow, I believe again.
>
> I am around enough other folks battling with MS and who don't know about Jesus, and there seems to be a kind of "hollowness" to their existence. They

talk about paying bills and getting a nicer kitchen or going up north—but that's about all. I think it's then that I most clearly understand that even in my wrestling match with despair, I have been given a grace to know a love—his love—that somehow, almost inexplicably, carries me through.

Since Audrey and I talked, I have been asking myself what I'm supposed to do with her story. It'd be great to have some absolutely real but simple bullet points about God's love that we can quickly take and apply to our own chronic pain. I desperately want to help us know how to understand we're loved by God, even when the data in our lives seems marginal at best and God's not saying a word.

But honestly, I don't know how to do any of that. And maybe I'm not really supposed to. Those of us who need this chapter most need warm, fuzzy conclusions least. What I can do is share some thoughts that have come to me as a result of entering a bit more deeply into my friend's tears and her struggle to find the love of God in pain that won't go away. It might feel a little more like rambling and a little less theologically tight, but in a way, that seems fitting. Like grieving with a perpetually hurting friend might call for an extra-long visit, a fourth cup of coffee, and patience to painstakingly dig for truth.

What first comes to my mind are the words of Jesus' half brother Jude: "Keep yourselves in God's love as you wait for the mercy of our Lord Jesus" (Jude 21). Jude's readers faced a ceaseless, cosmic battle as they struggled with the forces of darkness in the late first century. Some had found nothing but deep trouble since they began to follow Jesus. Others were even destined to die for their faith. Jude could have said anything to encourage these desperate believers. But what he chose to say is, "You're going to need the love of God to endure the battle. And you're going to have to fight hard—desperately hard—to keep yourselves planted under the influence and protection of that love as you wait for Jesus to return and end all pain."

Jude wasn't suggesting we fight to keep God loving us—God loves each of us eternally and unconditionally. But what Jude was saying is that in the midst of the battle, we must fight to allow the power of that love to be the centering focus and prevailing influence in our life. In John 15:9, on the night before his crucifixion, Jesus calls his eleven closest followers to essentially the same crucial task: "Brothers, you've got to abide in my love!" (author's paraphrase). Ironically, just a few moments later the soldiers came, and the disciples' lives immediately entered a period of long-term pain and suffering. How did they survive? How did they persevere and overcome? Why didn't they eventually turn their backs on a God who claimed to love them but had a seemingly sick, sadistic way of showing it? I think Jesus' disciples remained faithful to the end because they fought to keep themselves in the love of the Father. They persevered because they fought to abide in the love of his Son.

This is what I see Audrey doing. Every day she wakes

up and wrestles with her doubt about the love her left brain believes is there while her curled right hand and lifeless legs shout, "No, it's not!" She fights to look back and see where she has clearly known and felt God's love in the past. She scratches and claws to see where his love is active right now, even when the signs of that love might seem small and insignificant. She fights hard to stay close to believers who are trying to love her in ways that let her feel the love of the Father. And she especially fights to keep her eyes on Jesus of Nazareth, who fought to keep himself in the Father's love despite knowing that same Father was going to sacrifice him on a Roman cross.

That's the second reality that moved through my mind as Audrey poured out her story. I kept thinking about Hebrews 5 and the image of Jesus running to the Father for sanctuary:

> In the days of His flesh, when He had offered up prayers and supplications, with vehement cries and tears to Him who was able to save Him from death, and was heard because of His godly fear, though He was a Son, yet He learned obedience by the things which He suffered. VERSES 7-8, NKJV

The word translated as *supplications* was sometimes used of someone needing protection from the bad guys—in other words, sanctuary—and it's used only one time in the entire New Testament. I sense the writer uses this particular term on purpose here to create an image of Jesus as a vulnerable, frightened Son, running from those who want to kill him straight to the house of his strong, loving Father. Jesus pounds on the door, pleading, begging, and shouting with choked-back sobs, "Father, they want to kill me, but I'm innocent. Please open the door! Help me, save me! I'm so afraid."

And all Jesus hears in response is silence. Silence from the Father who at his baptism called him "beloved Son." Silence from the Father Jesus knew "was able to save him from death." Silence from the Father about whom Jesus had just said to his disciples, "When you all abandon me, I won't be alone. My Father will be with me" (John 16:32, author's paraphrase). Silence from the Father who "heard" Jesus but didn't deliver him until after he had been mercilessly tortured for hours and hours. And yet Jesus still addresses him intimately, with deep affection and trusting surrender: "Abba, even if you won't deliver me from this unjust death—not my will but yours be done" (Mark 14:36, author's paraphrase).

Maybe Jesus knew something about love that some of us struggle to understand. We're used to a love with props— physical comfort, medical care, government protection— and we forget that real love, God's love, still must be experienced in a world absolutely ruined by sin. A world that is profoundly broken and at war with the powers of darkness. Maybe Jesus knew about a kind of love that lives and flourishes in that kind of world. Love deeper than circumstance and more profoundly true than even our seemingly unanswered prayers. Love that doesn't always give us what we want exactly when we want it but loves us thoroughly nonetheless. Love that reveals its deepest character not when it bails us out of our pain—but when it comes close to us in our pain and weeps with us all the way home to our final, promised deliverance. Maybe Jude is calling us to keep ourselves in that kind of love. And maybe it is this kind of love to which Jesus submitted that night before his crucifixion— the absolute embodiment of that love to all of history and to each one of us.

And yet, a few hours after bowing the knee to a love deeper than feelings, Jesus cries out, "My God, my God, why have you forsaken me?" Doesn't this cry reflect our human confusion about finding the love of God when the hurt won't go away? Audrey believes in a love from God that is deeper than her circumstance—and then some days she doesn't. And the fully human Jesus, "tested in every way as we are" (Hebrews 4:15, HCSB), also had to fight to keep himself in the love of a God who abandoned him to the cross.

That day we talked, Audrey said to me, "Kevin, what's happening to me happened to Jesus. How could I ever think it couldn't happen to me as well?" I think she's beginning to sense that the Father is not only calling her to follow Jesus into his wounds, but calling her to live out Jesus' response to those wounds. No wonder the author of Hebrews calls Jesus a "high priest who [can] empathize with our weaknesses" (4:15). When we feel like the door is being slammed in our face one more time, we can run to him. He won't just advocate for us to the Father—he will hold us and our pain close to his heart and say, "I know. I've been there too. I'm a man of sorrows, acquainted with the deep grief you're feeling right now."

The call to this kind of "deeper than feelings" love is the bottom line not only for Audrey but for all of us who are honest enough to admit that we, too, have unexplainable, lingering wounds in our lives. God wants us to rest in a love that is beyond being defined by our comfort or even what we think we want or need. The point isn't to seek some kind of inner nirvana where the pain no longer matters. Instead, the Father seems to be calling us to experience a love that is deeper than our very real, most intense, continuing, and unexplainable suffering.

Peter spoke about surrendering to this kind of love in his closing words to suffering first-century believers:

> Humble yourselves, therefore, under God's mighty hand . . . . Cast all your anxiety on him because he cares for you.   I PETER 5:6-7

We're going to face a whole lot of stuff that we don't understand and don't feel we deserve—and some of it isn't going to get fixed no matter how hard we pray. It's going to scare us and make us doubt God's love. But we've got to surrender to a God who isn't just sovereign but who loves us and cares deeply for us, even when our enduring pain shouts that he doesn't.

I want to experience a love relationship with my God that would allow me to say, "In spite of everything, he is all to me." But I'm not sure it's even possible to know this kind of love without our "love props—those things that comfort us or make us feel safe—" being yanked out from under us. Seriously, can we hope to experience this deeper-than-feelings love of the Father if we continue to believe his love means always answering our prayers for the things we want, even good stuff like health, safety, a solid career, or a happy family?

When Carla's dad was killed by a drunk driver one night more than twenty years ago, she cried, "Kevin, I've asked God for years—could you please just let me have a conversation with my dad before he dies, an intimate moment where he would be vulnerable and share his heart and tell me one more time how much he loves me, like he did when I was a little girl? And now I will live until my own death with the pain of never again hearing those tender words from him. I know God loves the world. But does he really love me? Was that kind of closure with my dad really too much to ask?" Then Carla's sister was taken from us two years ago after a horrifying two-and-a-half-year bout with breast cancer, and we're still tempted to question, "Father, you took Paula, and now we have to live with the never-ending pain of missing her—do you really love us?" Even as I write, my youngest daughter, Caroline, a brilliant professional dancer, might be facing career-ending surgery and the death of her childhood dream. We're begging God, "Please no, Father," but the question remains: Does the reality of his love for us depend on his answer?

You might think I've got this all figured out and I'm giving you my mature, thoughtful conclusions after years of theological reflection. Not so. I'm just beginning to believe and live into this more deeply after wrestling with God for decades. Knowing Audrey and walking with her on her journey of long-term pain and shepherding many others with persistent wounds—not to mention my own long-haul battle with life—is moving me toward a cautious conclusion: If I don't surrender to God's call to live more fully in a love deeper than feelings, the foundation of God's love in my life is only one extended tragedy away from crumbling.

In fact, what if those of us who have our "love props" taken away are, like Jesus, being called to a profound Kingdom privilege? Because it is exactly this kind of love, lived through our wounded, surrendered life, that most powerfully reflects the Father's love. Audrey hates this thought because there's a part of her that doesn't want that kind of "privilege"— she just wants to be healed. And I'm certainly not standing in line asking for this "severe mercy." I'm simply asking the question. Is there a deeper kind of love that, when lived out in surrender to the God of love, is the most powerful display of his love in the universe?

I'm also wondering if God, through Audrey, isn't gently confronting us with the only two choices we really have. We can start fighting to surrender to this kind of love and live with hope. Or we can play into the enemy's hands, continuing to live the understandable but hopeless role of abandoned victim. Please, don't hear these words as unfeeling. And if you're saying to yourself, "You don't know me and my situation," you are absolutely right. But I can promise you—I care about your pain. Deeply. And when I suggest that there are only two choices, I'm not flashing easy-answer theology. I'm simply speaking a freeing truth with as much love as I humanly have to offer.

It's impossible to "make" ourselves experience this kind of love, but I'm convinced we can choose to offer ourselves to it. We can choose to make our hearts available for our Love to come to us. Otherwise, maybe by default, our seemingly never-ending suffering will lead us to offer ourselves to equally never-ending doubt, bitterness, anger, and despair.

This is the only love that can bring each of us all the way home. So I'm praying for Audrey and alongside Audrey—and I'm praying for myself. I'm also praying for you with deep compassion and tears for whatever wound you have courageously faced for so very long. I'm praying that God would grant each of us the courage and grace to allow our lives to become more and more about our longing to be with him, and that we would keep struggling to love and be loved not for what he does for us but for who he is and for his sake. I'm begging God to help each of us learn to love him in the night.

And at the end of this chapter, where I have tried to wrestle the best I know how with the so-very-difficult reality of Audrey's life, my life, and the lives of so many others—and with a God who says he loves us still—I commend a fellow-sufferer and his truth to your heart: "I feel that such distress,

distress that has forgotten even its name, that has ceased to reason or to hope, that lays its tortured head at random, will awaken one day on the shoulder of Jesus Christ."[10]

Or in other words—home.

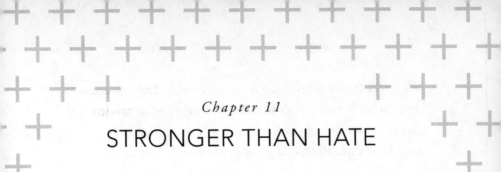

STRONGER THAN HATE

I have also decided to stick with love, for I know that love
is ultimately the only answer to mankind's problems . . . .
I have seen too much hate . . . and I say to myself that hate
is too great a burden to bear. I have decided to love.
DR. MARTIN LUTHER KING, JR.,
FROM HIS SPEECH "WHERE DO WE GO FROM HERE?"

I [pray] . . . that they may all be one; even as You, Father, are in Me and
I in You, that they also may be in Us, so that the world may believe
that You sent Me . . . and loved them, even as You have loved Me."
JESUS, JOHN 17:20-21, 23, NASB

I FIRST MET Marc Carlson around Christmas 2005. He and
his wife, Diane, came to volunteer at an event we hosted for
the families of Michigan prisoners through Prison Fellowship.
The Carlsons were new to our community, and it touched
me that with no coercion or manipulation, they just showed
up and jumped in to serve. What touched me more was
watching Marc immediately walk to where our Angel Tree
volunteers were taking pictures of families to send to their
incarcerated loved ones and kneel next to one of the children

who was patiently waiting his turn. He struck up an obviously affable conversation with this child who was twenty-five years younger than him, his very posture communicating love and humility and a simple desire to be present.

I was also moved because Marc is Caucasian and the youngster was African American. And even though our church community is diverse and as followers of Jesus we are so obviously called to view every human being equally as a son or daughter of God, I knew then and know now just how racially wounded our society—and the church of Jesus Christ—still is. So when a white guy I don't know walks into a ministry setting where most of the folks are people of color, I make no assumptions. In fact, I'm usually on edge—I know from experience that a whole lot of the racial insensitivity in America lives in the so-called majority, often simply because we've never had to personally deal with feeling marginalized due to our culture, our accent, the shape of our eyes, or the shade of our skin.

It wasn't until eleven months later, when I was baptizing Marc, that I first heard just a bit of his journey—and was moved to my core. On that morning, Marc stood in front of our community of faith and boldly said, "Hi, my name is Marc Carlson. I'm married to Diane. I'm an accountant. But I'm also a former white supremacist. And I'm here today because I'm no longer filled with hate. I believe in Jesus Christ, and he's in the process of completely transforming my life."

From where I stood next to Marc, I had a clear line of vision to the side door of the stage where the baptismal candidates lined up. Just about the time Marc said "white supremacist," I saw Samson (the brother from chapter 5) standing there waiting his turn. *I'm getting ready to baptize a former hardcore racist and one of the strongest and angriest African American men I've ever met—back to back—in the space of about five minutes*, I thought. And so I did. They both went down into the water and came back up in the name of Jesus Christ. The audience roared with delight. They always do. I think it's probably because baptism shouts, "Death and pain don't win!" And the people watching feel that victory not only for those in the water but for themselves as well. They're passionately screaming their triumph right up in the face of the forces of darkness: "You thought you had us, but our Christ beat the grave! So go back to hell where you came from, because we're now safe and alive in his strong arms!"

But as I look back on this particular baptism, I'm wondering if the folks in the crowd were cheering for yet another reason. I'm wondering if there was something about these two ideological enemies standing side by side, drenched in the water of Jesus, that represented some larger hope for a more cosmic kind of healing. Think about it: If Samson and Marc had met even a couple of years earlier, their hearts would have been filled with rage and fantasies of killing each other—Marc because of a stereotyped hatred of dark skin and Samson because he was angry at the world and understandably had zero tolerance for Marc's racism. But on baptism day, Marc and Samson were brothers. They were together.

They were at peace for one powerful reason: the love of God in Jesus Christ.

So maybe when the folks in the audience looked at Marc and Samson, they didn't just see Marc and Samson. Perhaps they saw Jefferson Davis standing arm-in-arm with Fredrick Douglass in the name of Jesus. Or Rosa Parks seated comfortably next to her new brother in Christ, the Montgomery bus driver. Or Emmett Till having a quiet, peaceable Sunday-after-church potluck with his Mississippi murderers. Maybe they pictured Hitler blessing Anne Frank or El Salvadoran Archbishop Oscar Romero bear-hugging his assassins. Or Crazy Horse and his band of Lakota Sioux sharing the Lord's Supper with General Custer and the 7th United States Cavalry. Or possibly they visualized Bosnians, Serbs, and Croatians weeping their repentance and forgiveness to one another, or the Hutus and Tutsis finally deciding to love one another—simply because of their own profound connection with the powerful love of God displayed in this One named Jesus.

In fact, I suspect that in the deepest heart-space of all, the baptismal audience that morning envisioned millions and millions of men and women—Japanese, Chinese, Korean, Puerto Rican, Mexican, Ugandan, Uruguayan, South African, German, French, British, Russian—you name it—with swords melted and reshaped into plows, kneeling in shalom before the reconciling cross of Christ. I believe they clapped and shouted at the top of their lungs because Marc and Samson, in that moment, gave them real hope for the healing of the festering racial and ethnic animosity that still seeps satanic pus into cultures, institutions, and personal relationships all across America and around the world. And maybe they were shouting about the hope they sensed for the healing of every relational wound they had ever had in their entire lives, shouting to God and for God—"We've got to have more of his love! His love in Jesus Christ is our only hope! His love alone can stop the bloodshed and heal the hate."

Whatever the audience understood that day, I want us to understand. I want the picture of Marc and Samson—and especially Marc's healing story to follow—to persuade us more completely than ever before that education, legislation, seminars, great sermons, and trying real hard cannot heal deep animosity and division. They can't stop wars. They can't even stop divorce or best friends from breaking up or parents and children turning on one another. And they can't stop self-loathing. Only love heals hate. Only love heals apathy. Only love heals the pain that divides. And there's only one love strong enough to heal like that: the love of God in Jesus Christ.

This is what God sent Jesus to do: to heal the relational division that has been Satan's main strategy for killing the life of God in us since he first convinced Adam to point his shaming finger at Eve, and jealous Cain to smash the skull of his brother Abel. The New Testament word is *reconcile*. God sent Jesus to reconcile broken relationships. Why? Because we're created in his relational image—Father, Son, and Spirit—and his primary plan has always been that we enjoy him and display him through relationship with him and one another. It only follows that our most crucial and deeply felt wounds will always be relational. Our deepest hopes and dreams will always be about continuing, deepening, healing, and reconciling relationships.

The same is true for people who don't believe in God. I promise, nonbelievers don't initially care that much about our doctrinal statement. They're created in God's image, so they primarily want to know if we can help them with their unreconciled relationships. They struggle just like we struggle—to not hate themselves and one another. Satan is continually destroying them relationally through gender misunderstanding and bitterness, through racial animosity, through broken families and friendships, and through self-loathing. They work hard and drink like fish and hop from bed to bed and from toy to toy because they are desperate, like us, to love and be loved. Nonbelievers long to love a God they don't know or understand, to love one another beyond their fears, and to love themselves beyond their shame. But they don't know how. And they will never know how—unless we actually display to them in living, miraculous, healing reality the reconciling love of God in Jesus Christ.

In other words, we have to do real church as Jesus called us to: living as a reconciled, loving-one-another community. The church cannot and must not be monolithic and homogenous. The body of Jesus must be for all people. As we love one another across divisions and wounds, we serve as the primary proof to a relationally fractured world that there really is a love in the universe that can heal us. N. T. Wright says the church was always meant to be "the worldwide community in which ethnic divisions [and, it's implied, all other divisions] would be abolished and a new family created as a sign to the watching world that Jesus was its rightful Lord and that new creation had been launched and would one day come to full flower."[11]

God didn't send Jesus to create religious clubs where it's all about a nice worship experience or well-spoken sermons or even cultural comfort. He sent Jesus to miraculously reconcile us first to God and then to one another so that we could live in miraculously reconciled communities demonstrating to the world that miraculous, healed, restored relationships are possible in him!

I hope we're getting this. God doesn't want us to know and feel his love so we can simply feel better about our day-to-day lives. Of course, as a good Father, he rejoices when his kids are set free by his healing love. And the stories in this book have been about how the experience of that love is available to every one of us. But there's more. He wants us to know his love so we can show that love to a relationally bleeding-out world. People are tired of empty words, but they will be drawn and healed by a love they can actually see and feel for themselves.

My sense is that for most of us, all these words about loving one another sound theologically nice and make sense— but it's so easy to nod our heads and go right back to what's comfortable. So let me say it again, in a way that leaves little doubt as to what I mean—and what I think Jesus means: Homogeneity, when intentionally applied to church, is an idea from hell. The New Testament never, ever calls us to intentionally be Jewish churches, Gentile churches, white churches, black churches, Latino and Asian churches, Pentecostal and Baptist churches, loud and soft churches, rich and poor churches. Our connection isn't primarily in culture, skin color, liturgical style, musical taste, or political background. Our primary connection is in Jesus Christ. Period.

Paul says that the very reason for the cross is not only to reconcile us to God but to reconcile us to one another (Ephesians 2:16). To settle for sameness, for comfortable homogeneity in the body of Christ, is to disrespect the purpose for Christ's death. To ignore God's call to love all of the one anothers in community isn't just an unfortunate oversight—it is to spit on the cross of his Christ.

Church isn't about your comfort level or mine. When the most powerful healing community in the universe functions like a glorified social group with a few Jesus slogans, a T-shirt, and a website, it sends the message that God and his love are anemic and that Jesus is sweet but doesn't have the power to do anything that really matters. When church becomes a place where we look alike, dress alike, talk alike, believe all the same things about everything, and basically mirror back and forth to each other how cool we are, then church shouts to the world, "You're going to carry your relational pain to your grave. There's no hope for healing. So deal with it."

Could it be that one reason unbelievers aren't quick to

listen to our words about Jesus reconciling us to God on his cross is because they don't see us living reconciled to one another? We're trying to get folks to believe that Jesus' death overcame the penalty of sin, and we can't even work out our cultural issues or love enough to hang with folks who like a different kind of music.

Our clear call, if we love Jesus and know we are loved by him, is to live out our identity as a part of a new family where everyone is literally and actually—not just theoretically and metaphorically—living as one. "Where there is neither Greek nor Jew, . . . barbarian, Scythian, slave nor free, but Christ is all and in all" (Colossians 3:11, NKJV). Anything less is fake church, pretend church. When we settle for pretend church, we're saying that our comfort means more to us than reaching our Abba's sons and daughters who don't yet understand. And we're sending a clear message to the world that we don't have what they need most.

We've become convinced that to come together and work through all the cultural stuff; old, deep wounds; and historical baggage—let alone personal hurts—is just too much to ask. And yeah, it's impossible—unless we're overpowered and saturated by a Lover and a love that won't quit and won't ever let us go. The reason we don't love well is not because it can't be done but because we don't yet personally know how deeply and powerfully we are loved. Remember Jesus' call: "Love one another . . . . *As I have loved you*" (John 13:34). I promise you, when God's love begins to break through, we can't help but love in such radical ways that the world will see the love and will absolutely know it comes from Jesus Christ.

For those of us who might be among the skeptical, consider the rest of Marc Carlson's remarkable story.

Marc grew up in Boston, Massachusetts, in the kind of middle-class community he describes as Pleasantville. Hockey was his first love. But he didn't have much of a spiritual life— he felt pushed into Confirmation and First Communion, which ultimately turned him against the church and all things "religious." Then, when Marc was in fourth grade, everything changed. His brother, who was four years older, started hanging with a different kind of crowd, a crowd deep into alcohol, drugs, and hate. As often happens with younger brothers, Marc followed his older brother, especially into the music. Marc said, "I listened to my brother's music every single day."

First it was punk—the lyrics were anti-society and all about hating life. Next came heavy metal and groups like Slayer, whose song "The Antichrist" is so full of pain:

All love is lost
Insanity is what I am
Eternally my soul will rot[12]

Look, I'm not trying to be overly analytical, but consider this: Marc, who grew up in "Pleasantville," had a nice family, and went to church, internalized this core message at a critical point in his life: "All love is lost. . . . Eternally my soul will rot."

Can you hear him? The enemy. The accuser. His poison-ous mantra is always the same: "He doesn't love you. And if there's no love for you, there's no hope for you." The enemy hates us all. He hates adults. He hates kids. And the way he hates us most effectively is finding some way, any way, to infiltrate our hearts and convince us that the God who loves us actually hates us and has left us behind. At the age of nine, Marc Carlson was overpowered by that lie.

Then, most devastatingly, Marc started listening to the music of the neo-Nazi movement, a group most clearly defined by how much they hate others. If what we feel inside is emptiness—and our emptiness is filled with shame and self-hatred—it follows that we will be ripe to hate those around us. When Marc shared his story publicly, in detail, with our church community, he told us, "The first neo-Nazi song I ever listened to was on the way to and from elemen-tary school." By the age of twelve, Marc was a "mailing list" member of the Ku Klux Klan.

"The message of the KKK took hold of me," Marc said. "There was no diversity in my world. I lived in an area that was 98 percent non-Jewish white, so all I had was the hate-filled message of neo-Nazi propaganda—and it began to shape me." Those seeds of hate that were planted at such an early age began to grow over the next fifteen years.

In 1997, Marc graduated from high school and saw, as he puts it, his "opportunity to explore racism further without my parents looking over my shoulder." By 1999, he had a hockey scholarship to Wayne State University, and Marc says,

"Believe me, without that scholarship, I would have never, ever come to a place like Detroit! Once I arrived, I was ticked off every day. I was angry at all the different cultures that were everywhere on campus—especially the African Americans and the Middle Easterners. I was even angry about the homeless folks I saw on the streets. In fact, as a middle-class white student, I felt like a minority myself. Detroit definitely added a whole lot of fuel to the racist fire in my gut."

Marc was smart enough to know that his beliefs weren't generally accepted, so he kept them "a deep, dark secret." But in these early Detroit years, he made a choice to dive even more seriously into the movement. He joined the European-American Unity and Rights Organization, the group led by David Duke, former Grand Wizard of the KKK. Marc was drawn to Duke's supposed desire to "clean up the Klan." In the next year or so, he attended several skinhead concerts, and in the summer of 2002, he went to an anti-Israel conference in Washington, DC. Marc says,

> I never condoned the murder of innocent people.
> But I had absolutely strong feelings about the
> superiority of whites and the separation of races.
> And—I hated African Americans and Jews.

Then, at the very depth of his obsession with hate, Marc met Diane. She was a serious follower of Jesus. He was an agnostic. "Our relationship exposed the worst in me," Marc says. "I was insecure and angry. I had begun to not want the hatred anymore, but I was stuck. Every single day, I would think, *I have nothing to live for.* I felt like I was in chains, like I was rotting inside. The only reason I didn't kill myself is because I didn't want my parents to be hurt."

Marc was a brilliant scholar-athlete with everything to live for, but inside he was overpowered by a heart that was empty yet full of hate. Like everyone else who doesn't yet know the love of the Father, Marc was a dead man walking. He couldn't possibly have guessed that everything was about to change.

In the fall of 2003, he and Diane finally talked about the painful truth of his life, and he shared his suicidal thoughts. It broke her heart and scared her to death. There was no quick fix to this level of pain, but she wanted to do something. So she bought Marc *The Case for Christ*, an apologetic book about Jesus by an atheistic journalist turned believer named Lee Strobel. Marc said, "Diane didn't understand the implications of giving me a book about a Jewish man. Jesus was a Jew, and I hated Jews!" But he read the book. And the thoughtful arguments about the person of Jesus being more than a mere man began to capture his mind and heart.

But Marc is quick to add, "Even more than that, what really started to change me was hanging with Diane's family. They were so full of grace, forgiveness, and love in the midst of a whole lot of personal pain. They gave and gave out of love to others, even when they themselves didn't have a whole lot to give. They had the joy and peace I craved."

By the end of 2003, Marc was ready to go to church for the first time since being coerced as a child. So late that year, he and Diane and her family went to New Life Christian Church in the Detroit suburb of St. Clair Shores. The first thing Marc saw when he sat down was a huge stained-glass window with a giant star of David right in the middle. Marc says, "Of course, I immediately wanted out! I put my head down because it hurt so badly. But I stayed."

And he went back. In fact, through 2004, he continued to date Diane and go to church, and finally he even stopped listening to racist music. At some point that year, he also asked Diane for a Bible. She gave him a modern translation of the Scripture on his twenty-sixth birthday, and Marc immediately began to read it.

Marc says, "From that moment on, I literally saturated myself in the Bible. And it's like the words and the stories and the truth—especially the truth I read in the New Testament—began to push themselves into my heart."

In Western Christianity we're so systematized, strategized, organized, and controlling, even about giving Jesus and his love away, that sometimes we don't get that God is pursuing each of us relentlessly with his love. Marc told us, "Finally, after a two-year journey with absolutely no set steps, God got into my heart. I believed in Jesus. Jesus, the Jew. And my rage began to heal. For the first time in my life, I began to have hope."

Pause just for a moment. Let this story sink into the doubtful, skeptical places in your spirit. You can't fake this stuff. Marc's hate began to heal without attending any seminars on race. He hadn't read any books on equality and hadn't participated in any self-help groups for rage-aholics or closet racists. There's nothing wrong with those things, but as Dr. King said, "Love is the only force capable of transforming an enemy into a friend."[13] King was simply quoting Jesus and his followers. Only Jesus' love can heal a multitude of sins.

This love of God in Jesus Christ can also heal the relational brokenness, the apathy, and the lack of forgiveness that might be residing in your own heart. This love is strong enough to heal even the hatred you've been afraid to talk about. It might not be hatred for another race or group but hatred for some-one who has hurt you, used you, devalued, disregarded, and discarded you and broken your spirit. But hatred longs to be healed. It must be healed. Left alone, hatred will continue to leak its bitter poison into your already wounded spirit, eventually sucking the life out of your relationships, family, and community and killing your chance to deeply love and be loved.

When Marc told our church, "For the first time in my life, I began to have hope," of course the crowd went crazy just like they did eight years earlier at his baptism. After the applause died down, Marc shared the next stage of his heal-ing with the Hope Community audience:

Diane and I got married, moved to Canton, and showed up here at Hope in the fall of 2005. We felt like we should be here, like this was the place for us—but I've got to tell you that my past wasn't fully healed. I had the message of reconciliation in my head but not in my heart. When I walked through

the doors of this radically diverse community,
I didn't hate others as I had in the past, but my
personal primary identity was still all about race.
But we dove into the community, and then I was
baptized, and my healing continued. Slowly but
surely I began to be literally transformed. Like it says
in Romans 12:1-2, my mind began to be renewed.
I began to see that the "new creation" Paul describes
in 2 Corinthians 5—was referring to me!

As Marc began to wind down his story, he shared a final picture about how drastically his life had changed. "Last year," he told us, "I went to Europe on business. I stayed a couple of days in Poland and spent some time at the infamous Auschwitz-Berkenau concentration camp. I thought I had a grasp on the Holocaust. I didn't. I should have gone twenty years ago." For a moment, it got very, very quiet in the sanctuary, almost as if we were all, including Marc, silently praying for the more than one million victims of Auschwitz's gas chambers. And as if we were also silently praying for ourselves.

Marc didn't say much more about his time at Auschwitz. It was like he knew that a more vivid description would somehow desacralize the moment. But Marc did quietly say, "This wasn't planned, but today I live in the most concentrated Jewish neighborhood in Detroit. And it just so happens that the amazing young woman who takes care of our three children is also Jewish."

Marc closed his story that day with these words: "I have been and am being transformed. I live with a freedom I never thought possible. All that garbage is almost a distant memory. I am a new creation in Jesus Christ." All because of the power of a love that covers a multitude of sins.

I'm reminded one more time of the main reason why I felt so compelled to tell Marc's incredible story. It's not just because it gives each of us real hope that God's love can heal our personal, relational mess. That's an important reason but not the main reason. I wanted us to vividly feel Marc's journey—because without living the love that changed Marc's life, the world has absolutely no hope.

I need to say it again: Without this love of God in Christ coursing through our wounded spirits and lived out sacrificially in the community of Jesus, the world will continue to bleed out. Marriages, families, communities, businesses, neighborhoods, nations, men and women, rich and poor, and every ethnicity—we will continue to hurt one another until everyone is simply . . . dead.

As I write, America is still reeling from the tragic, "opposite of love" human violence and death in Ferguson, Baltimore, Charleston, New York City, and South Carolina. Of course, legislators are throwing bills and laws at the pain as if a package of enforceable rules is the elixir for our hate. Educators are just as rabid about their new programs to help folks understand why we need to "just get along." But let's be honest. History tells us it can't work. We passed civil rights legislation in the sixties that obviously needed to be passed, and I honor the many who sacrificed to see equality in writing, to know at least that it's illegal in America to act out hate. Then in the seventies we took diversity training, and much of the material was profound and deeply helpful. But none of these efforts could ultimately kill the hatred living in so many human hearts. Looking back on the civil rights era, a whole lot of folks say, "It's over. Getting together was a nice thought. We passed laws and marched for justice at great personal risk and sang about peace. We were so hopeful. And we tried so hard. But the pain and division is still there, so now we're done. Have a nice life on your side of the fence, and I'll see you in heaven."

Just in the last week I've wept in my heart with an Asian sister in Christ who feels she has spent her entire young life justifying her Korean existence; a group of twentysomething university sisters who are so weary of being misunderstood, sexualized, stereotyped, and judged by men; and a young married couple on the verge of divorce due to broken trust and all kinds of other pain. Just today at the gym the news flashed on the TV screens that there had been another shooting in another theater—two dead, nine wounded. That report in the wake of five young soldiers shot the previous week in a military recruiting office. The world is broken. And dying. If we think anything but the love of God in Jesus is going to heal our perpetual, seeping, death-dealing, hateful, relational wounds, we're delusional. We're flat-out ignoring Jesus Christ. Marc's story—in fact, all these stories—aren't just about us healing. They're about us healing in order to heal the world.

Remember this—Jesus promised. He guaranteed if we love all of the one anothers as we are loved, no matter the cost, the whole world would know. They may not all believe, but they will all know—not just that we are with Jesus but that Jesus comes from God (John 13:34-45; 17:21-23).

A couple of years ago, a bunch of Hope folks were enjoying a barbecue moment on the front porch of our church, which is located on a main thoroughfare in Detroit. All of a sudden a Detroit bus driver pulled up in front of the building—stopped right in the middle of his route, opened the door, and asked me with a huge smile, "Hey, is there a plate of that barbecue for me?" When I nodded, he quickly fired one last question, something like, "Who are all these people, and why are they hanging out together and having such a good time?" Since he was holding up traffic, I quickly replied, "Well, we're a community of Jesus followers, and we actually just love each other." Yes, I really said that. And I knew I could say it just like that because I sensed that what the man saw from his driver's seat was absolutely our real love.

The bus driver said—and I remember his words because they stunned me—"Are you kidding me? All these different kinds of people? Together? In a church? Never, ever seen that before. I'll be back."

Precisely what Jesus promised. Love one another and they'll know.

Love can heal you and every deeply hurtful relational wound inside you. Racial wounds, wounds from your mom or dad or kids, wounds from your ex-wife or ex-husband or that close friend who abandoned you or that church leader who shamed you or the family member who abused you. God loves you so much and longs to heal you. Only his love can heal you—and heal the world. Your broken heart is waiting. A broken world is waiting. Choose his love. It's time.

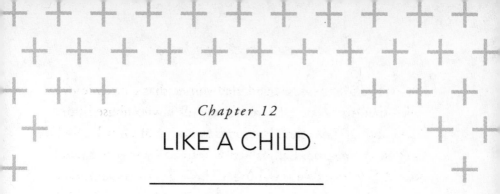

Chapter 12

LIKE A CHILD

_____

It's you I like. Every part of you.
FRED ROGERS, "IT'S YOU I LIKE"

Let the little children come to me . . . for the
kingdom of God belongs to such as these.
JESUS, MARK 10:14

I MISS MY three little girls—terribly—every day of my life. It's not that I don't love them now that they've grown up. Of course I do. Grown-up Andrea, Leigh Anne, and Caroline are tremendous human beings—they care deeply about people and live their lives with purpose and passion. I couldn't be prouder of who they have become.

But I sure do miss them as little girls. They were so creative, and they laughed all the time, and their faith . . . how do I even describe their faith? Their faith in a deeply loving God was spontaneous, trusting, and unflappable.

When Andrea was four, she rode with me to take one of my elders home from a meeting. When I dropped him off, I said, "Take care, brother." Andrea said, "Daddy, he's not your brother." I explained to her how we were special brothers because we both believed in Jesus. She looked at me and without hesitation offered, "I believe in Jesus, Daddy." When I gently asked her a few questions to make sure she wasn't simply trying to please me, I realized this kid truly, innocently, and sincerely believed in a Jesus who loved her and gave his life for her. Deep, spontaneous, childlike faith.

My middle daughter's faith in the love of Jesus was so strong that she would constantly write me notes when I was rushing to this meeting or that airplane—I actually think she "felt" my anxiety. One day when she was about ten years old, she slipped into my hand a colorful note that simply said, "God loves you, Dad! Love, Leigh Anne." I was obviously struggling in my grown-up, "save the world" pastor self to believe his love was big enough to take care of me that particular day—but little girl Leigh Anne had no trouble believing it for me.

As for my youngest, Caroline, I remember putting her to bed over and over between the ages of one and two. There was a picture on her wall of a blonde little girl in pink footie pajamas—who looked remarkably like Caroline—kneeling and praying by her bed while Jesus knelt closely behind her, his face right up close to hers. I would rock Caroline and sing to her, and before I laid her in her crib, I would point to the picture on the wall. "Who's this?" I'd ask. She would say in her eighteen-month-old way, "Cay-o-yine." And then I'd point to Jesus and say, "And who's this?" With finger in mouth and blankie by her cheek, she would reply in a tiny, sweet, slobbery voice, "Jshesush." I would whisper in her ear just how much Jesus loves her and how he would always love her. Just then it seemed she would sink into my arms and bury her head deep into my shoulder almost as if now, safe and secure in Jesus' love, she was finally ready to go to sleep.

Better than any commentary, these three snapshots of my very young daughters—and their ready faith in the love of God for them—illustrate what I think Jesus was getting at when he said that only those who become like children can enter God's Kingdom (Mark 10:13-16). I wonder if Jesus' words that day in first-century Israel—as kids, parents, and families listened—imply a further truth: that the perspective of a child isn't just needed to enter the Kingdom but also to function with any kind of power and effectiveness in the Kingdom. There is something about life and often about growing up that steals our ability to retain childlike faith in his love. And when we lose touch with his love, we've got nothing. We're in the Kingdom, but our hearts are empty (Ephesians 3:19).

It was ten-year-old, childlike Leigh Anne who handed forty-year-old, adult-like me a note that reminded me of God's deep love. I believed in that love when I was very young—but because of the deep pain of life over the years, as a grown-up I started to doubt and often flat-out disbelieve that same love. So the question begs to be answered: How does my adult self get back what Leigh Anne's childlike self so obviously and easily possessed? Jesus seems to be calling us to reclaim a childlike trust in God's great love for us, but is it really possible?

Jesus' words aside, some might be asking if it is even necessary to reclaim that childlike trust in God's love. "Of course adults see things differently than children do," we might say. "We see things now as they actually are." *Really?* I wonder. For sure we see and understand some things as grown-ups that children might not see or might not be able to fully process. But what if our problem is that we think that "the truth" we now know about pain negates "the truth" we thought we knew about God's love as kids? We believe the lie that our childlike view of the love of God can't coexist with our adult-like view of the pain of life. Our "adult eyes" have been so wounded that we've lost the "childlike eyes" we were never intended to lose. I fully believe that alongside our adult ability to see the pain of life, we are also absolutely intended to see the great love of God for us—like a child.

But how do we heal our eyes and reclaim our ability to see and feel the love of God like a child? Honestly, I wish I had a complete, definitive, and "easily lived into" response. I don't. But what I can tell you is what Jesus actually did to help heal the wounded, distorted, adult-like vision of his twelve disciples.

By the way, don't forget that their wounded adult vision wasn't just personal—it was cultural. In the ancient world, compared to grown-ups, children didn't matter very much. So, to show how precious and invaluable children are in the Kingdom of God, more than once Jesus placed a child in the middle of his followers. And then, in so many words, Jesus said, "Take a long, close look at this child. Because what this child has, you need."

That's what I want to do in the rest of this chapter. I want to place right in the middle of our conversation, for all our wounded eyes to see, one of the dearest sons of God I know. His name is Keith Brown, and, ironically, as far as age goes, he's not a child. He's sixty-four years old. But here's the truth: Because Keith was born with what some would call "special needs," he's been able to grow up to see and feel the pain of being an adult—while also being graced with the incredibly special gift of never, ever losing his ability to see and feel the love of God as a kid. Keith's childlike heart—his way of experiencing the love of God with simple trust despite much pain— has helped heal many in our community, including myself.

Listen long and hard to his story. Take a deep, close look at his life—because what Keith has, you just might need . . . to help you come home.

I honestly can't remember the exact day I laid eyes on Keith. But it was probably one of the first Sundays after we bought the church building on the corner of Marlborough and Jefferson on Detroit's tough eastside. I do vividly remember our very first Sunday worshiping in our new building. I remember walking up the front steps of the entrance and noticing that the flowers we had planted the day before in the stone pots around the church porch . . . were gone. And then I remember grabbing the handle of the metal door and seeing a fresh bullet hole in the aluminum frame. I can so clearly remember feeling overwhelmed and ill-equipped, wondering how we were going to be redemptive and effective in the name of Jesus Christ in this new, challenging community.

The day I met Keith, he was standing on the sidewalk out in front of the church, almost as if waiting for me to arrive. He gave me his huge, authentic smile, which I've only seen leave his face about three times in a decade. His speech was repetitive and not always very clear, and he was forward and shy at the same time—and his attention span wasn't very long. But he jumped in immediately and began to help anywhere and everywhere he could. In those early days, we were a willing but pretty disorganized group of believers just trying to find our way, and Keith literally dove right in beside us. From that first day, he has served, loved, and looked out for all of us, each of us, nonstop in his strong, faithful, yet childlike way.

Over the years through conversations with Keith, but mostly with folks in our community who knew him before Hope, I was able to piece together a few elements of his story. But the main source for many of the particulars I am about to share come from Keith's sister, Pam. She graciously agreed to sit down with Carla and me—and, of course, Keith—a few weeks ago. We talked for more than two hours and could have shared for many more as we laughed, cried, and marveled at the details of grace in Keith's remarkable journey.

Keith was born in 1951 and grew up on Philadelphia Street between 12th (now Rosa Parks Boulevard) and 14th, just a few blocks from where the Detroit riots erupted in July 1967. Keith was the fifth of nine boys born to a mother who worked hard as a nurse's assistant to help support her large family. Right across the street lived a woman I find hard to describe because there simply aren't too many like her—one of those silent heroes who loves long, deep, and sacrificially in the most desperate of conditions. Carla and I knew her simply as Mama Summers. Mama Summers was a human compassion machine fueled by love, willingly receiving the wounded who were so easily drawn to her. She and her husband managed a few apartment buildings around Detroit, including the one directly across the street from Keith's home. Pam was their only biological child. Keith calls Pam his sister not because they are actually related but because they've known each other since childhood, and he has grown to love and trust her deeply—a love and trust Pam shares for Keith as well.

The physical, spiritual, and emotional needs of the area between 12th and 14th were intense and felt by everyone in the neighborhood. Mama Summers' heart seemed to bleed most for the children. She took in kids for years and years, all without any help from the state. "Young, often teenaged mothers would get overwhelmed and come to my mom," Pam said. "So she would take in sometimes four or more kids at a time, babysitting until these child-like moms could come back to get their babies."

Pam recounted:

One time a woman with two kids came to my
mother with no shoes, no money, and no place to
stay, which was a problem not just because everyone
needs shelter but because in those days you couldn't
even get help from Social Services until you had
an address. My mother managed the building, so
she told one of the staff to "get a bed and make it
happen"—and so they did. That's just the way my
mother was.

I asked Pam how many kids Mama Summers had personally "mothered" over the years. She looked up at the ceiling
for a moment and then said, "Around seventy-five, I sup-
pose." So much love tenderly given away by one deeply caring woman, one life at a time, in a city filled with so much
pain. It was a love I'm convinced eventually helped heal and
launch my friend Keith.

One of the events Mama Summers organized for the children was affectionately called "tot-lots." She would take an
empty lot in the neighborhood, the city would deliver box
lunches, and the kids who may have had nothing to eat that
day would show up for a meal. Afterward Mama Summers,
who loved things tidy, would tell the kids, "We need to pick
everything up to make it nice for ourselves." One day during
one of these "tidying up the neighborhood" moments, Keith
came around. He was maybe nine or ten at the time. And

Keith helped Mama Summers sweep the street. She paid him for it, and from that day on, Keith kept coming back.

It wasn't about the money. There's something about Keith's innocent spirit that seems content with not having more and more and more. But, as Pam said, "Keith doesn't just have a kind spirit, he also has a keen sense of discernment. If he likes someone, he does. If not, then they're no good." Then she laughed and said, "And often his predictions turn out to be right." Without a doubt, Keith felt Mama Summers' love—especially her love for the children in the neighborhood—and maybe that day as she slipped him a few dollars, her love compelled him to return. Pam said,

> Soon Keith was my mother's right-hand man. He began to help with the younger kids, and he was the only one who could calm the spirits of the children—especially the babies—who were so deeply upset.

So many times I will be praying for someone at the front of the church after a worship service, and all of a sudden I will feel a hand on my shoulder and sense a hand on the other person's shoulder. Both hands are Keith's. During the most tearful, tender moments with someone who is in great pain, Keith just shows up. It's like he feels the wound, no matter where he is in the building. He brings his childlike faith and trust in the healing love of God—and healing happens. Every time he places his hand on my shoulder, it feels like healing happens inside of me. And usually while I'm praying, I can hear Keith just over my shoulder, murmuring over and over, quietly and respectfully, with his own unique pronunciation, "Jesus, Jesus, Jesus . . . " And then, often even before the prayer is finished, Keith is gone.

I'm convinced this healing way of being is part of the Holy Spirit's gift to Keith, but I don't think his gift could be used so powerfully if he didn't have the heart of a child. Because like a child, Keith doesn't overanalyze anything, especially when it comes to folks who are hurting. He doesn't worry about what people think or how he will be received or whether he can really help. Keith simply feels the pain and responds out of guileless compassion. And God moves. Just like Jesus said he would.

Keith watches for hurting people in and around the community, and he brings them to me. He simply takes them by the hand, and for some reason they don't refuse him even though they can't possibly know where he is leading them. Keith tugs on my sleeve and mutters his view of the required connection, and then he walks away, leaving the two of us to talk or pray or do whatever we need to do. Keith is like another pastor. Special education all his life, can't read or write much, no ministry training, and very limited verbal skills—and yet our Keith is a grown man who knows and gives away the love of God through his childlike heart.

Back to the '60s and Philadelphia Avenue—Keith kept on hanging out with Mama Summers and the rest of the family, including Pam. He would go on patrols with Pam's dad in the buildings the Summers managed and continued to help Pam's mom with the children. Pam said, "Keith and I got very close, but he became my mother's shadow." Mama Summers eventually asked Keith's mom if he could come with them to their summer church camp in Dexter, Michigan. During this part of Pam's storytelling, Keith immediately came alive at the word *camp*. "They had a swimming pool, they had a swimming pool, had a swimming pool, I went swimming," he said in his typical staccato style, with a huge smile.

Young Keith came home from camp and told his mom he loved it. Soon he was spending the night at the Summers' home, and as Pam said, "It was around that time that family with the Summers began. It was like one day Keith just never left."

Make no mistake—Keith's biological mother loved him very, very much. But I suspect that not only did she have her hands full providing for eight other sons, but she could see that Mama Summers' love was literally changing Keith's life. Some of the changes were noticeable and remarkable.

I've referred a few times to Keith's difficulties with speech. But once you get to know him, you really can understand him—and he really does like to talk! So much so that sometimes when I'm preaching and I pause during a sentence, Keith fills in the blank with his own words. Keith is following so closely that he will shout out a term—and often it really isn't that far from the word I was going to say. And if Keith doesn't know any other word to use, he'll usually just shout "Jesus." None of the other listeners in the sanctuary seem bothered or thrown off. In fact, I think they sort of like it, especially when he fills in my sentences with Jesus' name, whatever the context. It's like Keith is reminding us that no matter what I'm talking about, it always comes back to Christ.

But what makes Keith's "co-preaching" so astounding is that he didn't used to talk at all. Keith was born with what is commonly known as a cleft tongue, and his family had no money for surgery. So Keith simply lived with his condition. A few years ago, Mama Summers told my wife, Carla, that because it was so difficult for him to be understood, he simply never talked. Then Mama Summers said,

> One Sunday morning in church when Keith was
> nine or ten years old, the entire congregation was
> shocked and blown away when silent Keith suddenly
> stood up and shouted with passion, "God bless
> Mama Summers!"

When I heard this part of Keith's journey, the only word that came to my mind was *miracle*. When Carla told Pam this story, Pam said, "My mother believed in the power of prayer, and her faith was contagious. I'm not surprised a manifestation of this in Keith's life was his sudden ability to communicate without an operation or therapy." So did God reach through the veil of eternity and touch Keith's tongue? Or was this miracle simply about the healing power of his love—through Mama Summers—opening up the heart and mouth of a little boy who had been afraid to speak? We'll never know. But Keith hasn't stopped talking since.

Keith's biological mom released him to the Summers' care when they moved to manage another apartment building in a different part of Detroit sometime in the late '60s. From that time on, Keith Brown lived with, loved, and worked alongside the Summers. He not only willingly helped his new family with their buildings but also had other jobs that he deeply embraced. As Pam described each particular place of employment, Keith joyfully editorialized in his wonderfully repetitious way. You could tell he was so pleased with himself for the work he did.

Keith just loves to help people. Keith genuinely and innocently loves to feel needed and included, to feel like he's contributed in some way to someone's life. I relish watching Keith helping folks around the church, especially with his "no strings attached" attitude. My favorite moment comes after he's helped this person and that person for a few hours and then suddenly declares, "I'm going home," as if to say, "I helped, I feel good about it, that's it, and I'll see you tomorrow." Because unlike most of us, who only see things through our adult eyes, Keith doesn't analyze whether he could have done better or made someone happier. He doesn't make it all about himself. He does what he does to help folks from his heart, and then he lets go.

Keith and I are often some of the last to leave on a Sunday afternoon after church, and I'm very aware that we often "leave" very differently. As my adult self walks away from the building, I'm already analyzing my sermon, wondering if it had impact, and thinking about the several people I prayed with, questioning whether I "did it right," and reflecting on who I might not have loved well enough or who didn't like our worship service. In other words, I leave with a truckload of adult, rather self-absorbed, analytical bondage.

But not Keith. As I walk to my car, I can see him out of the corner of my eye, sauntering down Marlborough with that perpetual ear-to-ear grin, freely greeting neighbors: "Hi, workin' man!", "Hi, lady!", "Hi, neighbor!" It's like he doesn't have a care in the world, as if he's laid the last four hours down and is now walking freely into the rest of his life. He's not attached to his performance. He believes God loves him not because of what he just did, but just because God does.

Sometime around 1975, Pam took a job with a nonprofit housing corporation on the east side of Detroit, and the entire family moved to a home on Marlborough next door to where Keith presently lives. And, of course, Keith went to work right alongside Pam, cutting lawns and cleaning lots for the council she helped lead. Sometime later Keith got hired at the hardware store on the corner just a block away from our church building, which is where he was working when we came to the Jefferson-Marlborough neighborhood late in 2005. Such was life for Keith for around thirty-five years— even after Pam got married and moved away.

Then one day, just a few years ago, Mama Summers went to be with God. No one knows if she had an aneurism and then fell, or if she first fell and hit her head and then had an aneurism. What we do know is that Keith was getting ready for church and went into the bathroom and found her. He picked her up and made her as safe as he could and then went across the street to their close friend Marsha, who called 911. But when the ambulance came, Mama Summers was already gone. I will never forget the funeral. Keith came to the front, sat down in one of the oak pews closest to the casket, and wailed from a place deep within his spirit. Others in the sanctuary were quiet, almost as if in respect for the depth of love between Keith and Mama Summers that would produce such longing, such suffering.

Children naturally grieve freely, without shame. So do those who allow themselves to become like a child. And our God, like the good Father he is, draws close to his kids in their pain. Though Keith would have trouble articulating exactly what he felt in his heart that day, I know beyond doubt that Keith's Abba embraced him intimately, stroked his brow, and whispered in his little-boy ear, "It's going to be all right, son. I've got Mama Summers. And I've got you, and I love you, and I'm never letting you go." Just as Keith calmed the crying babies in Mama Summers' building on Philadelphia Street, Keith's God calmed Keith's childlike spirit and eventually, after a time, began to heal his broken heart.

My sense, and the main reason I was so excited to tell Keith's story, is that God wants to offer the same healing to you— if you will just for a moment set aside the adult lens through which you may tend to see your life. Be present to the child who lives inside your heart. Listen to what

your inner little girl or little boy is really feeling, really saying, and then offer that wounded child's real truth to your
Abba. I suspect there are plenty of tears in your heart—
perhaps locked away in your spirit for years—that long to
be authentically wept. You won't cry alone. Abba will come,
and if you let him, he will embrace you and weep with you.
And begin to heal you.

But I know how stuck we get in our adult mind-set. And
I know that even the most wounded of us might be pushing
back right now—hard—against the authentic, vulnerable,
healing, but potentially frightening path to which Keith's
life is calling each of us. You might be saying, "Touching
story. Keith seems like a wonderful man. But your framing
of his journey and our potential healing is 'inner-child psy-
chobabble' and not the Word of God."

Believe me, I understand your concern. I took five years
of Greek and two years of Hebrew at university and seminary so I could know—as sure as one could know—what
the Book says. The seminary I attended for four years has a
worldwide reputation for focusing on the literal, grammati-
cal, historical—and thus accurate—rendering of the text. I've
also grown up with the fears of the late modern and early
postmodern evangelical church about "straying" from biblical truth. I get it, I'm deeply concerned about it, and I'm on
it. But I'm also absolutely convinced that what I'm describing
is a healing that the Scripture is all about. This very morning
before I began to work on this section of Keith's chapter, I
just happened to open the Old Testament to Psalm 22:

You are He who brought me forth from the womb;
You made me trust when upon my mother's breasts.
Upon You I was cast from birth; You have been my
God from my mother's womb. Be not far from me,
for trouble is near; For there is none to help.

VERSES 9-11, NASB

It's fascinating and deeply instructive to see David—
Israel's strong, grown-up warrior king—remembering, in a
time of great danger and potential trauma, the nurture and
care of his God when he was a child. He chose to see his
life through childlike eyes and vulnerably invited God to
care for him in the present. This is exactly what Keith does,
almost naturally, that allows him to so deeply feel the pain
of others without fear, to serve without accolade, to grieve
without embarrassment, and to live present to each and every
precious moment, knowing that he is loved by God. Keith
is simply a grown man who has been graced to never lose
touch with his childlike heart. And this is the loving call of
God on each of our lives—to freedom. For just a moment,
stop analyzing and take a risk to feel. Respond to the call of
Jesus. Maybe it's time to follow Keith's lead and ask God for
the courage to become more like a child. Because when you
reclaim that child inside your heart, you take a step toward
home.

As I close Keith's chapter, I can't get the image out of my
mind of Jesus placing a child in the middle of his disciples
and saying, "Look, and be healed." I encourage you to take

one final close-up look at the life of this beautiful, childlike grown-up man. *Look, and be healed.*

Keith comes down front at the end of a Sunday morning service and stands by Carla and me. Boldly, with enviable childlike lack of self-awareness, he sings off key and claps off beat from deeply joyful places in his heart. I don't know what others feel when they see him in those moments, but every time I see Keith's guileless heart praising God in unselfconscious joy, I get tears in my eyes and realize anew just how much I want to come before my Abba with the same shameless, open-hearted security and happiness.

Our Hope treasurer, Katherine, tells a more behind-the-scenes truth about Keith:

> Keith gives financially every single week. Maybe he's missed two or three Sundays in ten years! Like a child, he carefully writes as best he can, "Keith Brown, $2," or sometimes, "Keith Brown, $5." Those dollars are the widow's mites. And I know what God does with widow's mites. God has used Keith to teach me about childlike faith and adultlike faithfulness.

Katherine went on to say,

> Keith became one of my favorite people when I asked him years ago if he would walk me to my car after the service because I had to deposit the offering that

day and didn't want to walk alone. And he did walk me—but not just that time. Now, every Sunday when I count the offering, he will ask me, "Pretty lady, ya got the money? Walk ya to ya cah? Walk ya to ya cah?" Honestly, Keith is my brother, and I just love him.

Here's a snapshot from Sue, our church secretary, who sees Keith almost every day:

Each morning, without fail, no matter the weather, Keith will walk past my office window on the way to the hardware store. He calls up to me, waiting for an answer—my signal to him that I'm all right. If he doesn't hear from me by the time he rounds the corner, he knocks on the front door and won't stop until I respond. It's his way of looking out for me— and in that moment I can see and feel my heavenly Father's relentless pursuit of me and how he doesn't stop either, no matter what—just because he loves me.

Gary Gentry, who with his wife, Becky, moved to Marlborough a few years ago and launched a ministry to kids called Hope House, says, "Keith is the very fiber of our community. He's pure of heart. He has found the Kingdom of God. I am so proud to call him my brother."

Wow.

Shalmar, who lives with her husband, Ben, just a few doors down from Gary, tells this Keith story:

When we first moved to the community, I started noticing that often our garbage cans would be brought back to the side of the house by the time we got home from work. At first I assumed it was our landlord, but then I was talking to Keith one day, and he mentioned something about our garbage cans and everything clicked. I shouted, "Keith, it was you!" and we both laughed. It's one of those seemingly small gestures that makes me feel so loved and looked out for in our neighborhood.

Imagine that. A tough, high-crime area of Detroit, with its share of drugs and violence—and a man armed only with childlike willingness to serve makes the neighborhood feel safer by taking garbage cans back to the sides of houses on pick-up day. I found out recently that Keith takes almost all the garbage cans back on the entire street, every pick-up day!

Perhaps no comment about Keith touched me more than Tricia's. She has been healing from her own wounded journey for many years and still struggles sometimes, like many of us, with shame. She said, "So many Sunday mornings I come to Hope just needing to be there. And when I walk in, Keith sets the tone of making you feel welcome and accepted—like God sees you and loves you."

Just think of it: a brother who was born with what society would term an "intellectual disability"—a tested IQ of around 68—and that brother "sets the tone" for the way an entire community of Jesus followers welcomes others in his name. No wonder Paul said "those parts of the body that seem to be weaker are indispensable" (1 Corinthians 12:22). He was simply echoing Jesus' words: "Unless you become like a child, you really can't be about My kingdom—at all" (Matthew 18:3, author's paraphrase). One of our deacons, Brian (from chapter 4), says it like this: "When I think about how valuable, precious, and irreplaceable Keith is, just as he is, I begin to believe that maybe it's true after all that I, too, have value just as I am."

Isn't this what we're all longing for? Underneath and driving all our pursuits—as valid and necessary as they might be—isn't there a longing to simply know we are "valuable, precious, and irreplaceable" to our Father? That he loves us. That he will never stop loving us. That he accepts us. That he has us in his strong arms. That he will never, ever let us go.

A few months ago during the morning worship service, our community collectively heard a thud from beyond the windows that separate the sanctuary from the foyer. In an instant, as we watched one or two doctors and a few nurses jump up from their seats and run to the back, information filtered to the front that Keith had fallen and was unconscious. For a moment, time stopped. People of all ages, races, and economic levels stopped everything, continuing only to breathe quietly in a collective silent prayer. What would we do without Keith—our brother who teaches us how to become like a child so we can allow ourselves to be loved and to love? Thankfully, on that morning, we weren't called to find out. The EMTs arrived, Keith regained consciousness, and the young medical technicians wheeled him down the left aisle of the sanctuary on a gurney to the door that leads to our wheelchair ramp. As we watched, Keith lifted his head slightly and looked over at all of us, and I think we were so stunned and grateful that many of us simply waved, reached out our hands as if to touch him, and gently called out, "God bless you, Keith," "We love you, Keith," "We're praying for you, Keith," and "Come back to us, Keith."

And one Sunday morning very soon after that, Keith was back on the front porch of our building, handing out bulletins and kissing cheeks, "setting the tone" for our fellowship to love, accept, and welcome each human being into the healing community of Jesus. He was back leading the way—with a childlike lack of awareness of leading anything—helping us all become like a child, helping us all find our way home.

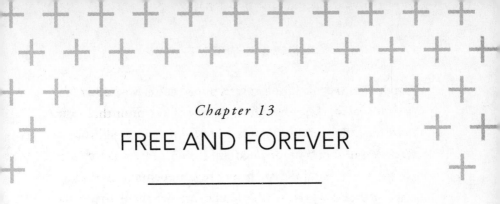

Chapter 13

FREE AND FOREVER

Very few people know that they are loved without
any condition or limits.
HENRI J. M. NOUWEN, *In the Name of Jesus*

For I am convinced that neither death, nor life, nor angels, nor
principalities, nor things present, nor things to come, nor powers,
nor height, nor depth, nor any other created thing, will be able to
separate us from the love of God, which is in Christ Jesus our Lord.
PAUL, ROMANS 8:38-39, NASB

IN THE 1987 fantasy adventure film *The Princess Bride*, the
young hero Westley is about to sail off to find his destiny
when he turns to his love, Buttercup, and says, "Hear this
now: I will always come for you." Understandably doubtful, Buttercup replies, "But how can you be sure?" To which
Westley responds with the deepest conviction, "This is true
love." Indeed.

Much more profoundly, these words echo our Abba's
words on every page and through every story in biblical
history. Remember his patience with repeatedly cowardly

Abraham? His constant forgiveness of adulterous, often ego-tistical David? The shocking picture of his prophet Hosea marrying the unfaithful prostitute Gomer as a sign of his relentless pursuit of disobedient Israel? Then there's the Cross, where God's Messiah says to unrepentant execution-ers, "Father, forgive them" (Luke 23:34). Paul made the astounding proclamation that our Messiah and the cross declare that nothing will ever separate God's children from his love (Romans 8:34-39). In all of it and so much more, I can hear our eternal God saying with tears in his loving eyes, "Here this now: I will always, always come for you—for this is true love."

Which brings me to the question—and the theme—of this chapter: But what if we never change? What if we work at allowing the love of God to heal us, but for whatever rea-son it doesn't seem to make a difference in the way we live? And what if I carry a significant piece of my wound, baggage, and sin all the way to the end because I simply couldn't—or wouldn't change? Does my God still love me—still come for me—then?

At first glance, this might sound similar to the theme of Cindy's story about the gracious love of God that leads him to forgive us. But this chapter and central story takes the love and grace of forgiveness to a new, scandalous level. The dif-ference has to do with choice. When we struggle to do right but fail, of course we need to know if we're still loved and for-given. But here we're talking more about a refusal to surren-der to Christ after we've believed in Him. This refusal might be belligerent, sort of an "I'm angry and frustrated with you, Lord, so forget you" kind of refusal. But it might also be born out of fear or weakness, anxiety or grief—in other words, more like "I refuse to surrender because I just . . . can't." Does God's love still come for us and cover us even when we say, "I believe in your Son, but I'm done trying to find healing and growth. I just can't do it anymore. In fact, I won't"?

Listen, I know the choice to refuse to surrender to the love of Christ has consequences. Sometimes these consequences are the natural result of disobedience, and sometimes they are about our Abba's loving discipline—loss of joy, intense loneliness, the pain of broken relationships, a wasted life, the loss of a degree of reward in God's Kingdom. There's nothing I want more than for sons and daughters of God to be so overwhelmed by his love that they live his healing, freeing, powerful life. But this chapter is for those of us who, for a variety of reasons, might never "get" the Father's love, at least to the point that it makes the intended difference in our lives. This chapter is for those of us who are terror-stricken that no matter what we do, we won't grow and change—and what we have always feared will finally turn out to be true: God really does love everyone else. But because of our choice to continue in our baggage and sin, he just won't—he just can't—keep loving us.

So let me share a bit of Eddie's story. I can't give you much background about Eddie because regrettably I don't know much about his journey before we met in late 2005. But once Eddie and I connected, we developed a close friendship, which created space for the part of his story I'm about to tell.

A few years back I was on the front porch of our church, just a few feet from the sidewalk, where hundreds of people walk by our building every week for all kinds of reasons. Some are catching the bus on the way to work; some are getting off and coming home. Parents and kids are on their way to the charter school a few blocks away. Some are probably on their way to get high or engage in some kind of nonsense. Still others are heading to the barbershop or the salon or the convenience store down the road, or maybe they are out to simply enjoy the weather and visit a friend. This particular afternoon I was on the front steps greeting folks, trying to engage willing passers-by in conversation. And then I saw coming toward me, stumbling more than walking, my brother in Christ and good friend Eddie. I approached him, we embraced, and immediately I smelled the booze. Eddie was so drunk he could hardly hold up his head, which kept nodding and drooping toward the sidewalk.

I had seen Eddie like this many times before because Eddie drank every day. There was only one time each week when I saw him and embraced him—we always embraced—and he hadn't been drinking. And that was when he passed through the Communion line at church just after receiving the body and blood of Jesus Christ. Eddie would take the sacrament from whoever was serving that morning and then walk right past me, usually wearing sunglasses, possibly to keep me and everyone else from seeing the red in his eyes. We would hug, and most Sundays I didn't smell alcohol. But most other days, Eddie would drink and drink and drink some more.

On this particular day on the street, I can remember pulling him close and asking, "Eddie, you know I love you, right? I want to make sure you do, because I want to ask you a tough question and I'm gettin' into your business, so are you cool?" Eddie was tracking well enough to nod yes and slur, "Sure, Pastor"—so I asked him, somewhat rhetorically, "My brother, do you know you're killing yourself with this poison?" Again Eddie mumbled yes, and then, with my arms around him, I followed with a third question, "Eddie, do you know how much God loves you, how much he cares about you?" He answered affirmatively one more time, "I know, Pastor, I know."

Honestly, I didn't believe him, but I also knew at the time that this was the kind of answer most folks are conditioned to offer in response to a question about the love of God. Seriously, given the fact that Eddie respected me and, even drunk, didn't want to offend me, what else was he supposed to say? The truth might have sounded more like, "Pastor, I obviously don't know God loves me because if I did, why would I be drinking my life away?" But Eddie simply did what many of us do when we're feeling empty inside. To protect ourselves, we lie and say something like, "Of course I know God loves me. Doesn't everyone?"

But the point of the story is what happened next. I can't remember my exact words, but I pulled Eddie off the sidewalk for a bit more privacy, and over by the massive tree that stands outside our building, I said, "I'm scared for you, bro. I'm afraid you're going to die. Do you want to stop drinking? Will you stop drinking? What can I do, man, to get you to stop screwing with your life?" This time Eddie paused for a moment, partly because he was so drunk and everything is in slow motion when your brain is saturated with that much alcohol, but also partly because I think he was contemplating—as best he could—an authentic answer. I'll never forget his reply because it was one of those "this is the real, hard truth, and what do I do now, God?" kind of moments. Eyes glued to the ground, Eddie muttered, half under his breath, "Pastor, to be honest, I don't ever plan to stop drinking—and no disrespect, but there's really nothing you can do about it."

And you know what? Eddie kept his word. He never did stop—until he died a few months ago, primarily from the long-term effects of murdering his body with alcohol. Remember, killing us is always Satan's end game. No matter what he dangles in front of us and how much comfort he promises us, he's always, always about taking us out. At the end, Eddie didn't even come out of his apartment much. Some friends and family regularly checked on him and brought him food—until one day he started losing control of his bodily functions and called a nephew, who came and took him to the hospital. But it was too late. Not long after, Eddie was gone.

Before I say much more, let me make something very clear: Eddie believed in Jesus Christ. That's why he sobered up once in a while and came to church and why he came to the altar to receive the body and the blood. If you asked him who Jesus was, Eddie would say, "The Son of God." If you asked him why Jesus was crucified, he would say, "For our sins." If you asked him if he believed in Jesus Christ as the Son of God who died for his sins, he would say, "Absolutely." But when I asked him—and I promise you, I asked him over and over—if he would stop killing himself with booze, he would always quietly, politely, and somewhat shamefully say, "I just can't." I even asked him once or twice if he would just pray for willingness to put down the alcohol, and he said he would and maybe he did. I'm not really sure. But what I do know is that this authentic believer in Jesus Christ never gave up the sin of excessive drinking—and furthermore, as far as I know, never got to the point of even being willing to try.

So, at the end of Romans 8, when Paul says that nothing can separate believers in Jesus from the love of God—was he talking about Eddie? Of course, the way Eddie's life played out wasn't what God wanted. It's always the Father's loving goal that we live long and free. He sent Jesus Christ for that very reason: to deliver us from every drop of sin's poison and judgment and to heal us from all of sin's consequences. But the reality is that for years of Eddie's life—at least for the decade I knew him—he simply didn't get it. So what does Eddie "not getting it"—or even being unwilling to "get it"—mean in light of God's promise that nothing would ever separate Eddie from his love? In the end, did God's love still come for Eddie?

What does the Romans 8 promise mean to Larry, who was a part of Hope a few years back and who died in much the same way as Eddie, for the same reasons? And for Rachel, who passed when she was about sixty but looked like she was ninety because of the impact of heroin, crack, and years of methadone? Each of these people clearly confessed their faith in Jesus to me and others and were a part of our church community. And what do I tell Steve, a believer who is struggling with his mental health and sexual identity, who's trying to receive the healing love of God and live righteously but not doing so well? In fact, he asks me regularly after he's screwed up—again—if he's going to hell. Should I tell him, "Yeah, Steve, if you don't eventually get your act together, there's no hope for you—God will be forced to kick you to the curb, forever." Or do I keep reminding him that his God will always come for him, because that's the nature of true love?

By the way, to be clear, I'm absolutely not talking about universalism. I agree with C. S. Lewis: There's got to be a place for those who in the end choose "not God." But that's not the case with Eddie, Larry, Rachel, and Steve. They believe in God and in his Son. They're simply children of the Father who have fought—and for the most part, lost—the battle to surrender to his love in the way they live their lives. So is God's love always coming for them?

My gut tells me that in the back of our minds many of us wrestle with our own version of this same eternal question. All of us are fighting something: anxiety, pride, jealousy, unbelief, fear, doubt, greed, lust, our tongue, an addiction of some type—fill in the blank with your own Romans 7 fleshly battle. If we're honest enough, we'll also admit that some days we don't even want to fight anymore, and for a minute or a week or a month, we also choose to give up and give in. And that same honesty will force us to confess that it's possible this fight will continue just like it did for Eddie—with varying degrees of success or failure—all the way home. If we have the courage to be honest, we wrestle with Eddie's question because we are Eddie.

True, our "sin of choice" might be more religiously acceptable than our brother Eddie's, and our moments of refusal to surrender might not be so obvious. But whether we grapple with the stench and ugliness of pride, greed, or hatred—or we die with a calcified liver, swimming in our own feces—the fact is we're not that different. We're all flawed and human, and even though we're "saved," there's also a part of us that won't be completely "saved" until we're finally home. That means in the meanwhile, we're all asking the same question: "If I struggle all the way to the end and sometimes even willfully choose to resist God, will the love of the Father still come for me?"

Many of us are absolutely terrified of God's answer. We're petrified that even if we believe in Jesus Christ and trust in what he did on the cross and not in our good works to atone for our sin—in the final analysis we will somehow prove by our inconsistent lifestyle or some unhealed flaw in our character that we are in fact damaged goods and deserve to be rejected. Forever. And the reason this fear must be boldly called out is because fear of rejection doesn't draw us closer to the arms of our God or help us to more deeply receive his love.

Instead, it pushes us further and further away. Why would I want to surrender myself to a God who in the end, because of my potentially still festering mess of a life, is going to reject me anyway?

Astoundingly, much of historic Christianity and even some of us have thought, *No, being afraid of losing God's love is a good thing!* We've mistakenly said, "Hey, no big deal. My fear that God's love for me might run out is helpful because it will motivate me to work even harder to please him. And in the end, he'll see that I'm worth loving and saving." Or we have reasoned, "Of course God doesn't want us to be paranoid about every little sin—but on the other hand, he knows that if we feel too secure in his love, we'll take advantage of him and live like there aren't consequences."

Listen carefully: It's not true. In fact, the notion that fear of ultimate rejection will motivate us to more fully surrender to Christ is a lie used by the enemy to keep us from the deeper intimacy with God we all long for. I've heard this "fear" argument for years and can quote you all the biblical texts for where this faux motivational principle allegedly comes from. And not only is the exegesis that draws this fear-based conclusion poor, but the entire premise is built upon a "straw man." Folks don't tend to run from scandalous, unconditional, everlasting love, and they don't tend to abuse it.

For example, we all know that kids respond to parental discipline so much better when it is delivered in a context of "you can never lose my love" than an atmosphere of "hey, if you don't obey, you're out of the family!" Similarly, children of God do not tend to say, "I know God is my Abba, and he loves me forever, and nothing I do will ever cause him to let me go—so I guess I'll flip him off and do what I want." The truth is, we run toward the kind of love that always comes for us because to know that kind of love is to at long last be secure enough to begin the healing process—to finally be on our way home. Jesus' follower John says it best: Fear doesn't motivate love because there "is no fear in love"; instead, "perfect love casts out fear" (1 John 4:18, ESV).

The reason Eddie never stopped drinking isn't because he felt so secure in the love of the Father that he decided to abuse his love. Instead, for whatever reasons—only God knows—Eddie just couldn't receive enough of the Father's love in the last decade of his life in order to be more thoroughly healed. But here's what I do know: The little bit of the Father's love that Eddie was able to receive is the only healing reality that got him off the streets and into the building Sunday after Sunday. It was the Father's never-ending love that brought Eddie's weary, booze-saturated body down the aisle every week to receive the body and blood of Jesus. Without that kind of love, I can promise you that the overwhelming shame of being an out-of-control alcoholic would have kept him far, far away. The last thing Eddie needed was the threat that if he didn't stop drinking, the love of God couldn't and wouldn't save him. Eddie didn't hang out at Hope because of the music or the sermons. He was drawn because of the scandalous, ridiculous, unconditional love of God.

Seriously, can you imagine if Jesus himself had been out in

front of Hope Church that day when Eddie stumbled drunk down Jefferson? Jesus surely would have put his arms around Eddie and asked him, "My brother, do you know you're poisoning yourself with booze? And Eddie, do you know just how much I love you? So please, I'm begging you, let me help you get sober so you can live." And then can you imagine Eddie telling Jesus, "No, Lord, I believe in you—but I'm too much of a mess to let go of the alcohol. I don't even want to. And there's really nothing you can do." And then, can you honestly picture Jesus backing off and saying, "Well then, bro, here's what you need to know—I love you, but my love only goes so far. If you don't eventually clean up your act, I've gotta cut you loose."

Nope. Never. Not the Jesus I know. Not the Jesus who talks about a Father who loves his rebellious son, the son who flips him off and flees to a far country, wasting his Father's money on hookers and staying far away for a long, long time. And when that same son finally comes to his senses and starts the journey home, the Father doesn't say, "Look, the young man who used to be my son has finally gotten his wreck of a life together, so I'm ready to make him my son again." Instead, the Father sprints down the lane with compassion, kisses, and gifts, shouting with the deepest, always-pursuing love, "My son—the rebellious son who has never stopped being my son—has finally come home! Let the party begin!"

How could Jesus make it any clearer? Even in his long-term choice to rebel, the son never ceased to be a son—even a beloved son! Because what Jesus knew to be true about the Father is that his love is always coming for us, no matter what. And don't forget, Jesus told this story to a wayward group of first-century Pharisees, tax collectors, and sinners, encouraging them to make their own journey home. Instead of threatening them with a frightening narrative about a Father who would cut them off if they didn't get it together, he calls them home to a Father who loves them against all reason—even if they continue to rebel. Jesus describes a love that is irrational, irreligious, and unthinkable, a love so comforting and securing that deep in our hearts, it's all we really long for. Indeed, all we really need.

The truth is, my brothers and sisters, what you absolutely don't need is one more threat, one more well-intentioned yet mistaken biblical interpreter, pastor, or teacher misconstruing one more overused text to frighten you into better behavior, one more ultimatum implying you can outrun God's love. What you need, what I need, what Eddie needed, what we all need, is a deeper revelation of his love, more profound demonstrations of his love, more scandalous announcements of his love that literally give us chills and bring us to tears because we can't believe he would love us that much, that deep, that wide, and that long. In Ephesians 3, Paul calls us to be "rooted and grounded" in love (verse 17, ESV)—to build our lives upon a love so foreign to our human understanding of love that it seems almost unknowable! That's why these days if I'm thinking about God's love for me and I'm not overwhelmed with, "No, Lord, you can't love me like that; it's too free, too forever, it doesn't make sense, no one loves like that—no one!" then maybe I'm not really talking about the love of my God. Some other god, perhaps. But not the God revealed to us in Christ.

After the night God graciously rescued me on the highway, he brought me Brennan Manning's *The Ragamuffin Gospel*. And these words helped me understand for the very first time that God's love is truly forever—and absolutely free:

> Because salvation is by grace through faith, I believe that among the countless number of people standing in front of the throne and in front of the Lamb, dressed in white robes and holding palms in their hands (see Revelation 7:9), I shall see the prostitute from the Kit-Kat Ranch in Carson City, Nevada, who tearfully told me that she could find no other employment to support her two-year-old son. I shall see the woman who had an abortion and is haunted by guilt and remorse but did the best she could faced with grueling alternatives; the businessman besieged with debt who sold his integrity in a series of desperate transactions; the insecure clergyman addicted to being liked, who never challenged his people from the pulpit and longed for unconditional love; the sexually abused teen molested by his father and now selling his body on the street, who, as he falls asleep each night after his last "trick," whispers the name of the unknown God he learned about in Sunday school.

"But how?" we ask. Then the voice says, "They have washed their robes and have made them white in the blood of the Lamb."

There they are. There we are—the multitude who so wanted to be faithful, who at times got defeated, soiled by life, and bested by trials, wearing the bloodied garments of life's tribulations, but through it all clung to faith.[14]

When I first read these words, I sobbed and sobbed. Even today, tears are coming to my eyes as I read about this list of human beings who are "me" and who know they are desperate for a love that will always, always come for them. These lines got Manning into trouble with some who thought he was subtly promoting Christian universalism. But those same folks might not have been so quick to judge if they had been honest enough to realize that they, too, were in dire need of this kind of radically unconditional love. It's so easy to be tricked by the enemy into holding on to a bit of our worthiness—sort of a Luke 18, "Thank you, Lord, that I'm not like this tax collector" point of view. I'm also pretty sure it's impossible to believe that this kind of exhaustive love even exists until we finally understand how personally desperate we are for it to be real.

This I can promise you: After the night of my almost suicide, if I would have read about any kind of love except the kind that is always coming for me, I would have eventually gotten back into my car and driven into eternity. Fear of my

Father's rejection killed my heart and almost killed me. What brought me back to life is finally realizing I could never, ever lose my Abba's love. This is the kind of love that also began to heal and is still healing Dan, Brian, Kennell, Melissa, June, Sophia, and Marc. And I believe with everything inside me that this kind of love is ready to heal you.

So let me say this to my brothers and sisters who have lived with fear of the Father's ultimate rejection for so long—it's time to let it go. Be honest. The fear has not helped you grow. It has not drawn you closer to your Abba. It has absolutely not helped you embrace his love. Instead, you have lived obsessed with your struggles and failures. Hell has distorted your image of the Father and caused you to believe that in the end, because of your unhealed baggage and long-term choices to disobey, God's love will not be coming for you. Listen carefully: That's a lie. Scripture says it's a lie. Nothing can separate you from the love of God in Christ Jesus. Absolutely nothing. Because of the cross, once you are the Father's child by faith in his Son, you are his forever.

What would it be like if by God's grace you could begin to believe, even with the tiniest mustard seed of faith, that the Father of Luke 15 even now loves "prodigal you"? What would happen in your spirit if you could begin to see him waiting, longing for, loving, and choosing you even when you have continued to not choose him? If you could understand that he yearns for that moment when he can burst through the door and race down the lane to smother you with compassionate kisses? And I wonder what would happen if you could just begin to lay down the frightening image of a Father who says, "I love you, but if you don't get it together, I'm going to let you go"—and begin to hear, ever so faintly, your real Father saying, "Hear me now, I will always come for you—for this is true love." That might be the moment when, mystically and wonderfully, as you contemplate a Father whose love trumps all, you come to your senses and begin your journey home.

One more thought about Eddie. Even with all of his unhealed wounds and often losing battle with his sin of choice, he was nevertheless a sweet and tender man. Once he shared with me about the recent death of one of his family members—maybe his brother—whom he loved very much. I listened for a while, and then we talked about Jesus and heaven and the hope of Eddie seeing his brother again. What happened next, I will never forget. Spontaneously, he leaned over, laid his head on my shoulder, and wept. And I remember thinking—underneath this alcoholic exterior is a wounded, broken man who desperately longs to be accepted, nurtured, and unconditionally loved. A picture, really, of each and every one of us.

I truly loved Eddie. He was my brother in Christ, a brother who simply couldn't and even wouldn't stop drinking. But his Abba loved him, even still. Honestly, though I'm obviously not Eddie's judge, when he died I'm pretty sure he didn't hear Jesus say, "Well done, good and faithful servant." And that makes me very sad, even sadder than the fact that his choice to continue drinking hijacked his potential, destroyed so many relationships, and in the end, shortened his life. But when Eddie entered eternity, I believe this is what he did hear from his Abba: "Surprised to be here, son? You shouldn't be. Because I promised that I would always come for you. For that is the nature of my true love." And at that moment, suddenly, everything Eddie couldn't "get" in this life about the Father's love for him finally became crystal, sparklingly clear. And the Eddie who told me years ago, "I'll never stop drinking, Pastor, and there's really nothing you can do about it," began an eternity of praise for a scandalously loving God who kept his promise to never let him go—and finally brought him all the way home.

Chapter 14

COMING HOME

The farther I run away from the place where God dwells, the less
I am able to hear the voice that calls me the Beloved.
HENRI J. M. NOUWEN, *The Return of the Prodigal Son*

But when he came to himself, he said . . .
"I will arise and got to my father."
LUKE 15:17-18, ESV

BY NOW YOU'VE probably figured out that, for me, the clearest and most moving image of the Father's love is Jesus' story of his prodigal sons. For the younger son, who kept trying to fill his emptiness with anything and everything in "the far country," the most important moment of his life was when he realized he was eating pig food and decided to finally go home. Or as Jesus says it, "When he came to himself." Recognizing his futile attempts to fill the emptiness in his spirit, the prodigal decided to turn his heart toward his father and his father's love. He got real and made the most important decision of his life: He chose to start his journey home.

Lory was sitting in her car one Saturday night on Jefferson

Avenue in Detroit. Her baby son, Jordan, was in the backseat. She loved him dearly, but Jordan was possibly the only redemptive result of a long-term abusive relationship with a violent criminal-type named Marlon. Even after Lory made it clear that she never wanted to see him again, Marlon forced his way into her house—and upon her—over and over. The control was not only physical but psychological. And though Lory was a professional—educated, accomplished, and very strong—she felt powerless to escape.

Lory hated Marlon and wanted him dead. Believing that he was too elusive and potent for even the police, she finally paid a guy named Mick five hundred dollars to take him out. That particular night she was parked across the street from the barbershop Marlon frequented. *If he shows up*, she thought, *I'm calling Mick, and my nightmare will be over.*

And then—she really doesn't know why—she looked up and saw a sign about fifteen feet in front of her car. It said, "Hope Community Church, Senior Pastor, J. Kevin Butcher." She was dumbfounded—because I had been her pastor when she was a kid.

Lory had come to Hope a few times while pregnant with Jordan when we were meeting at another location. But in the last year, she'd lost touch with us—and with God—and she thought maybe God and his love had lost touch with her. But then she saw the sign. *What are the chances*, she thought, *that the barbershop of this violent, hateful man happens to be across the street from the church pastored by a man who I know loves me and is safe? And how is it that on the very night I try to finish off my abuser, I happen to park directly in front of the church sign?*

We sat down together one evening a few weeks ago so she could tell me the rest of her story. "When I saw your name, I decided to not do anything else that night," Lory told me. "The next morning I came to Hope." At the age of twenty-nine, deeply wounded Lory, daughter of God and believer in Jesus, "came to herself" and chose to take her first challenging step toward her true home.

I want to tell you the rest of Lory's story, but be forewarned: Her story is heartbreaking and in some ways maybe more painful than any I've told yet. But Lory's slow but sure, courageous odyssey toward the Father's house is exactly the one to close with because I want everyone—no matter how deep their pain and how long and difficult their road—to have real hope that they, too, can not only choose but keep on choosing to move toward the Father's love.

At first glance, it might seem difficult to understand how Lory found herself in such a damaged and dangerous position that night in the fall of 2005. She was raised in a home in the Detroit area by Christian parents who met her material needs. She went to church and youth group and sincerely believed in Jesus as a child. She was also an A+ student and a member of the student council in high school. At least on the outside, Lory's life seemed like typical, reasonably healthy middle-class American fare. But appearances sometimes lie. Behind the scenes, little girl Lory was feeling the impact of hell inside her middle-class bubble. Lory told me,

When I was young, my dad smoked weed and drank, and when he was high or drunk he was volatile and angry. My mom was crazy codependent with my dad and with almost everyone else. I knew my parents loved me, but my family simply didn't feel very safe.

And then there was the sexual abuse. A slightly older son of family friends began to "do things" to Lory as early as five or six years old. Hearing her account of the invasion of her sexuality, against her will, at such a tender age, broke my heart in ways I can't really explain. This abuse went on and on, all the way through her early teens. Even on trips with the church youth group. Sometimes he came after her despite having another girlfriend. Sometimes he involved his friends. "I didn't know how to make him stop," Lory said. "I had so many confused feelings—not only were our families 'church friends,' but when I was really little, I thought I was in love with him and wanted to marry him. I had no idea how to sort all of that out."

When Lory was sixteen, she walked in on this young man in his home while he was watching violent porn—and he raped her. It was a devastating wound that propelled Lory toward a slow-death kind of lifestyle that plagued her for much of the next fifteen years.

A part of her death march involved alcohol and eventually drugs. Lory's grandfather was an alcoholic and had a bar downstairs in his home, so one night she stole a beer, drank it, and liked it. Around age fourteen she began to drink and eventually use drugs with her friends. She told me,

> The only way I made it through adolescence was to try to have "family" with my friends. They were a crowd of very angry kids—angry at society and especially the "institution" of high school. We also hated people who seemed fake, phony, and happy all the time. Once, after doing acid, we even developed a hit list of people we wanted to kill. I had another group of friends like this who were also in my church youth group. In fact, I first smoked pot with these church kids on a youth trip to Florida. I rolled my first joint and took it in with me to Disney World and loved it so much I never stopped.

Then, in September of her senior year of high school, something violently pushed Lory toward full-blown addiction and an even more intense level of spiritual and emotional suffering. During a trip with a girlfriend to a university in Wisconsin, Lory sat down next to a guy at a party, and he bought her a beer—a beer Lory believes he spiked. That began a nine-hour nightmare of powerlessness, physical violence, and repeated rape. Of course, she tried over and over to get free and even faked needing to throw up once in order to try to escape. But her captor smacked her around and kept carrying her back to the room until she was rescued by a couple of good men who thankfully saw what was happening. Lory shared,

I never told anyone anything until maybe the
following summer. But this I know: Without a doubt,
this is the incident that broke me. Things escalated
after that. I was completely out of control the rest of
my senior year.

By the time she enrolled at a small Midwestern Christian
university, Lory was an addict. Why a Christian school? Like
some of us reading this chapter, Lory believed in Jesus but
was completely disconnected from experiencing his love—
which led to her misguided, desperate attempts to fill the
emptiness and heal the brokenness. But she still believed:

I fell asleep every night as a kid dreaming I was at the
manger with baby Jesus. Even in high school, when I
was a mess during the year, in the summer I went to
a Christian camp as a counselor. No one knew about
my issues because I was an A+ student from a camp-
connected family, so everyone thought things were
cool. And I sincerely tried to help kids spiritually at
camp even when I was a mess myself. I even waited
to party till the weekend.

The camp also had some counselors who were students from
the Christian university Lory ended up attending. She told
me, "By this time I knew the life I was living—and lived all
throughout high school—was killing me. I thought, *Maybe
this Christian school can be my first shot at rehab.*" The strategy

worked—to a point. Lory stopped drinking and using—yet was still living with a seriously damaged spirit. But she didn't know it. "I didn't think much about healing my first two years in college because I really didn't believe I was wounded," she said. "What had happened to me was bad for sure, but I mistakenly thought it was just part of what women had to endure." So, she says,

> I tried to fit in. I lived in the cool kids' dorm and had a cool-kid boyfriend whom I thought I was going to marry. I even made it through in three years because he was older, and I didn't want to still be in school after he graduated. But the problem with trying to just "fit in" was that all the other kids seemed "pure," and I knew I wasn't. I had to pretend my way into purity. And for two of the three years, it all worked out pretty well. As for Christianity, I avoided the fake God that can be so common in a religious school and really tried to live my faith—and in some sense, I believed God was with me.

But the house of cards that was her sincerely attempted sobriety finally came crashing down. I think Lory would say her relapse was almost inevitable because not drinking or using, without much-needed inner healing, usually doesn't last.

> My third year at school I watched ten guys who were my buddies get kicked out for using drugs. I took

their expulsions personally because I knew I wasn't different than them. Even though I had been clean, they were me. I delivered newspapers to the school, so one day I took the papers and burned them in protest in a public place on university property. Soon I was near expulsion myself. At one point I got so angry I threw a table at a professor and was ordered to go to counseling if I wanted to stay. So I went. I got kicked out of the off-campus house I was living in because they thought I was doing drugs like my friends, even though I wasn't. But I ended up finding a room in the small town just north of the campus . . . and the room was above a tavern.

You can guess what happened next. The unhealed pain came pouring out almost more violently than before. Lory lived above the bar for three months, most of the time feeling "completely alone and ostracized." Finally, she broke up with her boyfriend, the guy she was sure she was going to be with forever.

When I got kicked out of the house I had been living in, I got drunk for the first time in over two and a half years. I also slept with a guy for the first time since high school. I told my boyfriend, and it turns out he had cheated too. So from that time on, I slept with anyone and everyone and told my school therapist it made me feel like I finally had power over men.

But of course it meant the opposite. It meant that men, even abusive men, still had power over her, a life-giving truth Lory learned later when she went to treatment.

Listen carefully—Lory was a believer in Jesus. She was raised in church and was a regular at youth group. She spent three years at a Christian university, going to chapel and doing expected Christian stuff. To use her words, she "fit in." But fitting in and doing expected Christian stuff can still be "the far country"—just as much as doing drugs and sleeping around.

After she graduated, Lory had a few brief glimpses of the Father's ever-pursuing love at a three-month leadership school in the mountains of Arizona. In one instance, she and a friend were stuck on a mountain in a storm that ended up taking several lives, and "we were desperate and reading the Bible, and miraculously, people we didn't know—people who loved God—took us in." And she knew God was with her. She said, "My entire time in the mountains, living in the wild and carrying only the things I needed, was a time of growth for me and God. But even then, I got bored and slept with one of the guys in our group." Like many of us, Lory kept trying to take a few halting steps toward home before her unhealed past and the emptiness inside locked her down once more.

In the fall of 1996, at the age of twenty, Lory began law school in Detroit. The next few years were about studying. And partying.

I was dating a decent guy who loved me for who I was. And honestly, at the time, I wasn't drinking.

But that September he was killed in a car wreck, and I felt lost all over again. I started drinking like crazy. I quickly found a new boyfriend, and we started getting drunk so much together it was toxic. And by the way, it wasn't hard to find booze—even though I was underage—because all the law school events had alcohol.

It was in September of 2000, after graduation from law school, when Lory met Marlon, the man who would abuse her for the next several years, almost to the point of madness. She met him on her birthday at her favorite Detroit eastside bar. The owner of the bar was a friend of Lory's who gave her "cheap joints and beer." He knew Marlon and knew that he was a drug dealer, hit man, and violent hustler, so he didn't want Lory to have anything to do with him. But Lory was intrigued and went out of her way to meet Marlon anyway. She knows now that this was a "far country" trap of the enemy, but at the time she was living on the edge and not listening to anyone. And then, in the spring of 2001, he demanded sex.

I told him no over and over, but then I was at the door of my house, and he was right behind me. I knew enough about him to know I needed to be afraid. He was a huge man. I knew he had killed people. He followed me in and raped me. And then he proceeded to stalk me—and show up at my door

demanding sex—for the next five years. My life
was practicing law, drinking and drugging to try
to escape the pain, and living in terror of Marlon's
next phone call, threat, or attack.

In 2004, Lory found herself pregnant with Jordan—by
Marlon—and she cut down on her drinking and smoking
weed well into the first year of her son's life. But then, after
a short time of relative peace, things with Marlon escalated
again. That's when she found herself outside the doors of
Hope Community Church, working up the courage to
have him killed. Instead, Lory finally chose to take her first
baby step toward home. She told me, "I thought to myself,
*I can't kill him. I can't do time in prison. Either I'm going to
get even more completely lost—or it's time to come out of the
mess I'm in.*"

In the next few months, Lory began to open her heart to
a few of us at Hope, and we began to journey together—but
she didn't stop drinking and using. Wouldn't it be sweet if we
only had to make one choice to get up, leave the far country,
and run to the Father's house? But we're in a spiritual war.
The enemy keeps scratching and clawing at our backs, always
trying to destroy us by luring us beyond the sound of the
Father's voice calling us beloved. Sometimes we find ourselves back in the far country and don't even know how we
got there. So we must choose again and again to move toward
our Abba, leaving anything behind that we've used to try to
fill the emptiness. Lory knew it was time to come home, and

her choice was real—but she wanted to drag a few "souvenirs" from the far country along for the ride just in case the "God loves me" thing didn't work out. Soon, tragedy—and yet another chance to choose—was on her doorstep.

In 2009, she started to date a young man who was trying to live soberly, but, Lory said, "I brought him back to booze." One night he drove drunk, got into a wreck, and died. At her boyfriend's funeral, Lory said, "I think I heard God actually say to me, 'Lory, come home.'"

She finally began to see and feel the consequences of where and how she was living. And for the first time in a decade, she really tried not to drink and smoke weed. "But," she said, "I also told myself another lie—that I could do this mostly alone as long as I had a little guidance and counsel from folks at church. I would literally take walks with loving brothers and sisters in Christ to talk about not using anymore—and I would be wasted while we walked!"

I talked with Lory a lot during this period and sensed her sincerity. For the very first time, she had begun to feel that there really was a God who loved her, and she desperately wanted more. But she found herself so very afraid to let go of the props she had used to survive. So even though her journey toward the Father was real, it was a path filled with painful landmines and setbacks. But a huge breakthrough—and even one more chance to choose—was on the horizon.

In January 2011, she went to a party hosted by her law firm, got drunk, and ended up falling down two flights of stairs. Banged up and embarrassed, she still tried to drive home, hit something on Wayne State's campus, and eventually needed to be driven to her house by the police. That was it. Lory was ready to make her most profound choice yet, admitting that though she had no power over the abuse in her childhood, she had power now as a grown daughter of God to choose a healing destiny. She let go of the last of her far-country security blankets and began the final steps of her journey to the Father's house. Thirty years after our child-hating enemy first assaulted this precious daughter of God, Lory chose to go to treatment.

The day came, and another sister in Christ and I picked Lory up and drove her to the train station. We prayed, Lory boarded, and the Father was waiting for her with his powerful healing love at the treatment center in Chicago.

> Treatment cleared the fog and got me out of denial about what had happened to me. I really used to think that abuse is just what girls have to endure. By minimizing and denying all those years, I only injured myself more, and there was no way I could heal. I drank and used in order to run from the hurt and the trauma. Now I know I don't have to run anymore.

While Lory was in treatment and even after she came back home, her relationship with God continued to heal. She began to learn things about the way God loved her that somehow evaded her in childhood church and even during her time at a Christian university.

When I first started to heal, I didn't want to hear anything about Jesus. I always thought he forgot about me. It was like God was supposed to be a little more distant, but Jesus was supposed to be close. So why didn't he stop stuff from happening to me? But I have learned that Jesus has always been with me. When I was being hurt, his arms were around me. He was taking the abuse into his own body before it ever got to me. He wanted the abusers to stop—but he gives everyone a choice, even the choice to tell him no. When I think about my past now, I literally see Jesus there with me in the pain.

After all these years, my abused, broken, and now healing sister can at last hear Jesus' voice gently whispering, "I love you." I'm going to use the word *miracle* again because I have no other explanation for Lory's healing transformation. I've never met anyone more wounded, and I've also never seen anyone fight God's love harder. For a long time, even after her initial choice to come home to the Father, Lory couldn't even cry. Her tears were buried beneath layers of defense and fear. When she perceived the slightest threat, Lory would understandably lash out as if to say, "You need to back off—no one is going to ever hurt me again." Now those outbursts are fewer, and the tears are more frequent. Today, even when she does react out of past-trauma-induced anger, she is more quickly and authentically repentant and usually reaches out to me or someone she trusts in the body of Christ for help on how to make amends and move forward. Signs of healing, signs that Lory has finally chosen to live her life close to her real home.

A few years ago, Lory had even healed enough that she was able to confront her former abuser, the gangster Marlon, and at last slam the door on that intimidating chapter of her life. That day was one of the happiest, proudest days of my entire pastoral life. I remember thinking, *Way to go, Lory— strong, healing, beloved daughter of God. Greater is he who is in you than he who is in the world.*

The enemy waged all-out war at Lory for three decades. And I promise I only told you half the story—Lory should be several times dead and gone, not only physically but emotionally and spiritually. Yet none of Satan's arsenal was a match for the healing power of the love of God through Jesus Christ.

But the bottom line is this: In order to access that healing love, Lory was called to choose. And choose. And choose again. In fact, she's still choosing. Lory's choice to keep coming home is still sometimes a "mixed bag" of the good and not so good. She told me, "Sometimes the trauma of my past still haunts me, and I feel like using would be so much easier." In fact, weed has been her most difficult battle. She let it go in 2011, but for a time it came back into her life. Often, smoking a joint will calm her anxieties and fears in a way that she feels nothing else will in the moment. But lately she said to me, "The weed's got to go. Again. It's time." One more choice in a lifetime of choosing the Father's love—the only substance in the universe powerful enough to "fill us with all the fullness of God." So is the journey home for all of us.

Toward the end of our time together, I said, "Lory, I've known you for a long time, and for years, your life was two steps forward and three backward. These days, it seems that you choose your Abba and his love more often than ever before. Why the change?"

She replied with conviction, "Because I finally know what I really want. I want to be filled with his love."

Perhaps Lory's story is your story. Maybe not in the details, but like Lory you've known you are wounded, empty, and desperate. Yet for years you've tried to find satisfaction and healing in a far country that has not only never healed you but instead has left you bleeding out. Perhaps you, too, are at a crossroad just like Lory was that night in 2005, sitting across the street from the barbershop on Jefferson, drowning in fear and ready to kill. Or again in 2009, mired in shame because her boyfriend drove drunk into eternity. Or once more in 2011, so high she fell down two flights of urban apartment stairs and almost died. Or maybe your crossroad isn't quite as dramatic. Maybe your moment of truth is simply about the years you've played Christianity's game of lying about what is really going on inside your empty heart. You're tired of believing in a God who seems like nothing more than a benevolent dictator, possessing the best set of rules in a screwed-up religious universe. You're tired of singing the songs and memorizing the verses and doing church stuff all while experiencing so little of the Father's love in your spirit.

Or maybe you're one who has tried to fill up your emptiness with a series of unhealthy relationships, a successful career, more money, the perfect family, constant approval, another degree, or addictive obsession with health. Yet in the midst of all your pursuits, you find your true self longing—still. Empty brother or sister, hear me: You don't need to live this way anymore. Lory's Father is your Father. He's healing Lory. He can't wait to begin healing you.

The enemy will lie to you: "Nice story. Nice book of stories. Nice thoughts about a loving God who calls himself Father. But it's not for you. You're too strong—or you're not worthy. Or it's just not your thing. Or whatever." This is the same lie Satan told Brennan Manning over and over some years ago, a lie Manning recounts in his final book, *All Is Grace*. It's a lie that baited this amazing son of God into believing that after his initial choice, he couldn't continue to choose the Father's love. So for years, in between speaking engagements and book signings, Manning chose instead to go to the far country, spending days trying to drink away his insecurity and sadness.

Sometimes it's still hard for me to believe that the man who first introduced me to the Father's love died prematurely from the long-term impact of alcohol because he couldn't accept that God's love was there, day after day, for him. Yet I *can* believe it because Satan is powerful, slick, relentless, and hates us all. Manning wrote his last book to warn us that we're not different—that our journey will end up just like his if we don't choose and keep on choosing the Father's love. Remember Jude's words: "Keep yourselves in the love of God." The Father's love is not going to magically sink down into your spirit simply because you've been moved in some way by a book of stories. You've got to choose—maybe for the first time or maybe the four thousandth time—to open your heart to a God who is desperate to heal you with his scandalous, unconditional love. He is waiting. He is longing. Don't waste another second. Take a step toward home.

That step might be as simple as falling on your knees in desperation like I did so many years ago, saying, "Father, I'm empty. I'm tired. I've got nothing left. Please, I've got to know that you love me. Show me your love." The journey always begins with that first choice—the moment when we come to our senses and say, "I will arise and go to my Father." So, beloved son and daughter of God, get up. Start moving. It's time.

As I bring this chapter—and all the chapters—to a close, I wish I could manufacture some fantastic, memorable, almost magical story that brings everything together, makes you cry, and ensures that you start moving toward your Father's arms. I wish with everything inside me that I could reach through these last pages and embrace you, look you in the eyes, and somehow convince you that your Abba loves you. I wish I could heal your wounds. I wish I could convince you you're not alone and give you courage to begin. I can't do any of that. But I can tell you one more time how much I love you—and share one final story showing that, twenty-five years after first choosing to go home to my Father, today I choose him still.

Several Sundays ago at Hope Community, we sang our praise for most of our two-hour worship service. One of the songs was "How He Loves" by John Mark McMillan, who penned the lyrics the day after the tragic death of his best friend. I sat on the front row of Hope's sanctuary and bellowed my favorite words:

> We are his portion and he is our prize
> Drawn to redemption by the grace in his eyes,
> If grace is an ocean we're all sinking. . .

And then—

> I don't have time to maintain these regrets
> When I think about the way
> He loves us, Oh how he loves us . . . [15]

And right about the first "Oh how he loves us," I fell apart. I wept not because I had stopped believing in the magnificent love of my Abba but because that morning I needed a fresh retelling of his love. I had been giving out nonstop for weeks. I was depleted and burned out. After a month in the desert, the words were a clear, life-giving stream. It was one of those moments when I felt the sheer rush of my heavenly Lover's embrace, and my head immediately found its way to my hands. I wasn't just a little weepy. I was wonderfully undone.

Pastor Rita sitting on my left saw my tears and placed her

sensitive hands tenderly on my back. Then Pastor Pam came from across the sanctuary and held me on my right. Soon Willie, my brother who just got out of prison after thirty years, came down front and knelt at my feet, positioning his strong hands my head. I think Cindy might have been there, too, and Dan and James and Lory—all of them praying for me while the larger community of Hope continued to passionately sing, "Oh how he loves us." And I chose to stay right there, in that moment, receiving the healing love of the Father through "good church."

I've got to tell you, in that healing moment Satan was still spitting his lie in my face—"Folks are going to think you're weak. Don't let them see you like this!" I came close to drying my tears, putting on an emotional mask, and quickly becoming Pastor Fake again. But these days I know that to not keep choosing, moment after moment, to reconnect with the love of the Father—is to choose death. I had to choose in 1990 after my near miss with a freeway embankment, and I had to choose several Sundays ago, and I must choose again today. No matter how far up in the far country I have been or how long I have stayed, when I choose to take a step toward him, the Father always runs to meet me. And immediately his love begins to heal my wounds, fill my emptiness, and set me free—every time. Because of my Abba, I am fully, freely, passionately, joyfully alive. That same Abba, with his strong, healing, freeing love, is waiting—for you.

So, to those who might be reading these stories, still stuck

in the far country yet desperately longing for the Father's love,
I leave you with a final invitation—through Lory's words:

> Be brave. Even though you don't know what's next,
> if you're sick of where you are, you must choose
> to go to the next place. You must choose and keep
> choosing—to come home.

EPILOGUE

Keep yourselves in the love of God.
JUDE 21, NKJV

Get busy living . . . or get busy dying.
ANDY DUFRESNE, *The Shawshank Redemption*

"DAN'S GONE," I HEARD A STRANGE VOICE SAY. It was the first Saturday morning in April, I was in the final stages of editing this book, and even though it was a number I didn't recognize, for some reason I decided to answer the phone.

"The police called, and it looks like an overdose. I thought you'd want to know."

All I remember next is the deep wail that came from my heart as I shouted, "No, no, no, no . . ." and then the grown-man tears and the pounding of my fist against the dining-room table and my wife rushing to hold me in her arms, crying with me until neither of us could cry anymore. Soon I found myself on the phone with one after another of Dan's brothers and sisters in Christ who loved him so much. Then I spoke with his devastated daughter, Corey—the same daughter who received communion from his loving hands that morning at Hope Community six years earlier, soon after Dan was released from prison.

Dan Schoenfeld—the man I hugged and kissed and in whose ear I whispered the love of God so many years ago at the Macomb County Jail. The man who believed in Jesus Christ almost a decade into his prison sentence and who allowed the Father's love to heal so much of his broken heart for years after that. The man who called me best friend, who traveled with me to share his story after his parole, and who worked alongside us at Hope, giving the healing love of God away to countless others.

Gone.

It would have been easy *not* to share this part of Dan's story. Most of you reading these words would have never known the tragic ending of Dan's life and would have simply believed that the love of God, mystically and without invitation, continued to heal Dan more and more completely until the moment of his ultimate healing. But that's not the way it works. The whole point of the Good News is that the Father's redemptive, healing love *is* offered to us in Jesus. But we must—we absolutely must—*choose and choose again* to receive it.

Remember how Jesus begged his closest followers, "Abide in my love" (John 15:9, esv)? And how Jude, his half brother, years later passionately compelled believers, "Keep yourselves in the love of God" (Jude 21, esv)? Listen, God's love *does* heal, redeem, forgive, and fill—*but we must choose*. Because the very moment we stop choosing to live in his love, by default we choose to fill our lives with other things and seek healing somewhere else—a "somewhere" that always leads to death. Not just physical death, but a slow, daily, piece-meal death of soul and relationships, freedom and joy, and absolutely everything else that comes from our loving God. The bottom line is that my friend, Corey's father, and God's precious son would be alive today—if only he had continued to bravely choose to abide in the Father's love.

One more thought. Dan didn't wake up one morning and suddenly decide to reject the love that was healing him. It *never* happens that way. Dan made a small choice here and another small choice there—and after a while, all the seemingly insignificant choices added up into larger choices. Then, when his wife died in tragic circumstances just six months ago, Dan was already positioned to dull his deep, understandable pain with the very substances that had *almost* killed him so many years before. The Father has Dan in his strong arms now. Of that I am sure. But oh, the pain and death that could have been avoided—and the life Dan could have continued to give away to a broken world—if only he had bravely continued to choose the love of a Father who called him a beloved son.

But . . . there's another way. Brian *is* choosing—not perfectly, but daily he seeks the love of the Father in his business, marriage, and ministry with men. I just got a text from Kennell, and he's wrestling hard to bravely choose that same love in some difficult circumstances on the west side of Detroit. Melissa and Phil invited me over for dinner a few nights ago, and even in the midst of normal "young mar-ried couple" struggles, I could literally feel the chosen love that is the foundation of their relationship. A few Fridays back, I sat for several hours with Samson in Milan Federal Prison, where he is battling more legal appeals and worse, daily violence—but is still choosing to hope in the love of God. Sophia is living into the challenge of getting her GED while the Father's love continues to heal her wounded relationships with her children and grandchildren. Dan's death hit June hard—at one time they co-led the prison ministry—but she continues to passionately live out the love of God with the prisoners and families he has given her to shepherd. She told me, "I'm devastated. But I'm not going to use." Nickola is slowly recovering after yet another bad auto accident and is being loved well by her Hope family. Elle and Cindy are flourishing in the love of the Father, and you can see it in the way they consistently choose to serve others in our community. Audrey courageously lives into the complexity of her challenging life, struggling to choose daily to trust in her equally complex Abba and his love. The love of the Father has healed Marc to the point that he now leads a small group of men into the experience of that same love—and he and his wife just had another baby. Dan's death also hurt Lory deeply—but it also moved her to get even more serious about living in recovery. And Keith? He's just Keith—not without struggle but choosing to believe with childlike faith that he has an Abba whose personal love for him is greater than all.

Listen carefully. Not one of these brothers or sisters is perfect. And they all continue to face serious challenges in their lives. But they are your journey mates on the path to the healing love of the Father—and each of them bravely and tenaciously continues to choose the love of God.

As do I. The last few days, in the midst of some of my own present confusion, fear, and struggle, my heartfelt prayer has been "I'm yours, Father. Show me the way. Keep me covered in your love."

The last Saturday in April, Dan's friends and family gathered at Hope to celebrate his life and grieve his untimely death. During the service, I kept thinking about Andy Dufresne's words in *The Shawshank Redemption*: "Get busy living . . . or get busy dying." I also kept thinking about *you* and how God loves *you* so very much and how he's waiting with open arms . . . for *you*. So, my brother, my sister, I'm asking you right now to join us. Choose his love. Take another step toward home. And live.

NOTES

1. Brennan Manning, *The Ragamuffin Gospel* (Sisters, OR: Multnomah Press, 2000), 45.
2. Sally A. Brown and Patrick D. Miller, eds., *Lament*, (Louisville, KY: Westminster John Knox Press, 2005), 17.
3. LeAnn Snow Flesher, "Lamentation and the Canonical Psalms," *The Living Pulpit* (October-December 2002), 36.
4. Robert Karen, "Shame," *The Atlantic Monthly*, February 1992.
5. C. S. Lewis, *The Lion, the Witch and the Wardrobe* (New York: Harper Collins, 2005), 169.
6. *The Green Mile*, directed by Frank Darabont (1990; Burbank, CA: Warner Bros., 2000), DVD.
7. Allan N. Schore, *The Science of the Art of Psychotherapy* (New York: W. W. Norton, 2011), 139.
8. C. S. Lewis, *The Magician's Nephew* (New York: HarperCollins, 1994), 116.
9. Maude Maggart, "How Deep Is the Ocean," *With Sweet Despair* © 2005 SMAX Productions, Inc.
10. Georges Bernanos, *The Diary of a Country Priest* (New York: Caroll & Graf, 1937), 53.
11. N. T. Wright, *Paul: In Fresh Perspective* (Minneapolis, MN: Augsburg Fortress, 2005), 157.
12. Slayer, "The Antichrist," *Show No Mercy* © 1993 Track Record Studios.
13. Dr. Martin Luther King, Jr., *Strength to Love* (Minneapolis, MN: Fortress Press, 1981), 54.
14. Brennan Manning, *The Ragamuffin Gospel* (Colorado Springs, CO: Waterbrook, 2005), 31–32.
15. John Mark McMillan, "How He Loves," *The Medicine* © 2010 Integrity Music.

IS AN IMPOSTOR ROBBING YOU OF GOD'S LOVE?

"Honest. Genuine. Creative. God-hungry. These words surface when I think of the writings of Brennan Manning. Read him for yourself—you'll see what I mean!"

Max Lucado, New York Times bestselling author